BEING
ESSENTIAL

BEING ESSENTIAL

SEVEN QUESTIONS *for* LIVING
AND LEADING *with* RADICAL
SELF-AWARENESS

DAIN DUNSTON

DISRUPTION
BOOKS

New York   Austin

Published by Disruption Books
New York, New York
www.disruptionbooks.com

Distributed by Disruption Books

For ordering information or special discounts for bulk purchases, please contact Disruption Books at info@disruptionbooks.com.

Cover and book design by Sheila Parr
Cover image © Shutterstock / elodea.proteus

Library of Congress Cataloging-in-Publication Data is available.

Print ISBN: 978-1-63331-059-9
eBook ISBN: 978-1-63331-060-5

First Edition

THIS IS DEDICATED TO MY MOTHER, NANCY BURRIS DUNSTON,
WHO TAUGHT ME TO VALUE THE QUESTIONS I ASKED.

CONTENTS

Everything that needs to be said has already been said. But since no one was listening, everything must be said again.

—ANDRÉ GIDE

LOOKING INTO
THE MIND *of a* LEADER

A LEADER STOOD IN THE hallway outside his office. Through a glass door, he could see across the elevator lobby to the other side of the building. Over there, through another wall of glass and, beyond that, a third glass wall, he could see three of his direct reports holding a meeting he knew nothing about. He thought about walking over to sit in, but he knew instinctively that he would not be welcome. And although he had only been in the job for three weeks, he knew in that instant that he was not going to succeed.

He had taken on the job of running operations for a fast-growing tech company because the new CEO, a client he had helped before with people problems, had called. He had some young, immature managers running sales and ops. He wanted to put them all under the leadership of a senior officer. He needed an adult in the room to herd them in the right direction.

"It will be easy," the CEO said. "You'll be great at it."

But it wasn't easy and he wasn't great at it. And the worst of it was he knew in his bones that this was a bad decision before he accepted the job, and yet he went ahead with it anyway. The offer of a few million shares of unvested stock would give him just the payoff he needed if the company went public. And why wouldn't it? The CEO was one of the smartest he'd ever worked with and had already taken two large companies public with great success. How could this fail?

There were a lot of voices in the leader's head as he stood in that hallway, looking through those three glass walls, a lot of voices with some not-very-helpful opinions. The voices had a few questions, like *What should I do now?* But the time for asking the right questions had been *before* he got into this position.

To be fair, the situation was probably stacked against him. It was a little like a slapstick comedy where the new stepdad joins a dysfunctional family and the kids are determined to see him fail. To be honest, he came into the role feeling so uncomfortable for so many reasons that he surely would have come across as inauthentic and even just a little weird. He also came in with a fixed attitude about the young managers, instead of an open mind and an open heart. And to be *really* honest, he had come into the situation carrying baggage from some personal issues he should have been home cleaning up instead of commuting to another city, trying to pass himself off as an up-and-coming tech executive.

He lasted, in total, only four months in the job. He left feeling crushed, humiliated, and defeated. He had no idea where to go next except to try to reignite his previous client base and generate some revenue. Yet, he was determined to find the answer to one burning question: How had he become so lost?

Maybe you can relate this story to your own journey as a leader and as a human being. Who among us hasn't found ourselves in the wrong job, or feeling that we didn't belong, or wishing we could stop making decisions that took us into dead-end career moves? I know that I've been there because the story I just shared with you is mine.

• • •

NAVIGATING YOURSELF IS THE WILDEST SEA YOU CAN CROSS.

I grew up with a father who was on the fast track to becoming a CEO by the time he was forty-five, and I knew, by age thirteen, that I did not want his life. So, it's ironic that by the time I was thirty-five, I was working in the C-suite as a speechwriter helping leaders tell their stories. When

I saw an executive deliver a speech, I knew I had to help them understand who they needed to *be* on stage. From that inspiration, I found a natural progression to helping them understand who they needed to be when they came off stage as well.

So the experience of failing as a leader at the tech company shook me to my core. How could I have lost my connection to who I needed to be? But the experience also fired me up to find out why I had made such bad decisions and how I could rewire my mind to be the awesome, inspiring human being I always wanted to be (but secretly doubted I was worthy of becoming).

I started reading everything I could about how the leadership mind works and soon discovered there was no such thing as a leadership mind. There is only the human mind in which we each live. The best leaders are simply those who are the best humans, with better access to positive mindsets that help them live creatively and authentically. They live with appreciation and humility. And they also live with a fire in their belly, a fire to make a difference.

I talked to people I thought could coach me through the process. If I was going to get back in the game, I needed someone who could get me into the kind of mental and emotional shape that defines the best players.

In Santa Fe, I reconnected with one of my oldest friends, Dr. Sat-Kaur Khalsa, a Sikh minister and psychotherapist. "You've lost touch with your spiritual self," she said. "You have to start there." And so I did.

In Austin, I was introduced to Dr. Frank Allen, a therapist and coach, who was to become my zen master (with a lowercase z). Along with his background as a psychologist and his work on understanding how the mind works, he is a grandmaster in two different Japanese martial arts.

In Boston and in Rome, in California and New York, I talked with some of the brightest minds I could ever hope to meet and watched as they modeled for me a new way of looking at life and living, a new lens with which to develop a sense of what I call radical self-awareness, so that whenever I wasn't thinking right (and it happens often, to all of us), I was able to catch myself—even laugh at myself with amused curiosity—and readjust the stories I was telling myself.

I also returned to my writing. I wrote a novel, *The Downside of Up*, which tracks a corporate speechwriter who lets himself be talked into becoming the CEO of a company, only to find that the investors are running some shady stock plays that could land him in legal jeopardy and leave 11,000 families without a paycheck. It's a comic, but very real, look at how the character has to retrain every part of his mind so that he can save the day. It was, in part, me rewriting my own story. And, in part, it was a journey for every reader as they reshaped their own leader's mind.

Just a year later, a former client brought me in to help with some challenges at a new company he had joined. My client said, "Something has happened to you. You're deeper now." I smiled and thanked him. He was right. I could feel myself radiating a new energy.

That same month, my old friends Kevin and Jackie Freiberg, authors of some of the best books on business thinking you'll ever read, called me up. "Let's find something to work on together," they said. They invited me to join them in writing a book called *Nanovation*, about low-cost innovation in Asia that was transforming the way some of the world's biggest companies bring products to market, products that not only changed the market but helped the companies who made them radically cut their costs. Vijay Govindarajan of Dartmouth College's Tuck School of Business called *Nanovation*, "Quite simply, the most practical book about innovation I've ever read."

THIS IS YOUR CHANCE TO REWIRE YOUR OWN LEADERSHIP MIND SO YOU CAN BE THE LEADER YOU KNOW YOU CAN BE.

I worked hard and, until writing this, never felt I had to share my Waterloo moment as head of operations at the tech company with anyone ever again. Did everything suddenly go well for me? Of course not. I'm a human being, which means I can bounce like a basketball if I'm not watching myself. But over time and with daily personal practice,

I rewired my mind. Along the way, I helped many other leaders do the same, from CEOs to those just starting out in their careers.

And now I'm presenting the work to you. This is your chance to rewire your mind so you can be the leader you know you can be. So that you can create a world you want to lead, a world you wish you could live in.

> We must be willing to get rid of the
> life we've planned, so as to have
> the life that is waiting for us.
>
> —JOSEPH CAMPBELL

WHAT DOES IT MEAN TO BE ESSENTIAL?

Everyone would like to be essential, as in "She's essential to the movie! We can't get funding unless she's the star." Or "He's essential to winning the game! When he has the ball, the team is unstoppable." Maybe this book can help you achieve that level of fame, fortune, and fabulousness. But what we're really talking about is something different.

This is a practice about being of the essence, of being true to your Essential Self.

You're on a journey to find your Essential Self so that you can experience—and share with the rest of the world—the heroic, masterful, deeply present person that you were born to be. The self that's been trying to get your attention since you were a child. The self who is ready to tell you who you are and why you're here, if you would but listen.

In a tree outside my house lives a mockingbird who comes every spring to sing. It's his way of capturing the attention of a potential mate. An individual mockingbird will sing as many as two hundred different songs in his lifetime. Some of those tunes will be shared with other mockingbirds, drawn from the morning cacophony of birdsong around them. Some of the songs will be unique to a few birds who echo various sounds in their habitat.

Each mockingbird sings a different song. Yet each mockingbird, in his essence, is the same as all the others.

So, what is the *essence* of you?

First, the bad news: you're not that different from anybody else. We like to think that our problems—and our best attributes—are unique. But the truth is, our traits and our challenges are similar to everyone else's. Line us all up in our varieties of sizes, colors, genders, orientations, beliefs, identities, and cultural backgrounds and we can look very different. Catalog your childhood experiences and your cultural associations and you can prove to the world that you have suffered in unique ways. Of course you have. Let me be the first to acknowledge your unique, individual suffering. But, like the mockingbird with his own unique collection of songs, you're just like all the other mockingbirds.

Now the good news: you're not that different from

anybody else. For every wrong, for every hurt, for every tragedy you have ever suffered, you can go out and find a million others who have suffered the same experience or, at least, their parallel version of it. Because of that, we can understand and support one another. The damage done in childhood, the tragedy of loss, the cruelty of systemic prejudice, the tyranny of violence, the horror of famine or fire—none of those are unique to you. You share those experiences with other human beings since the very dawn of human time. Sometimes we hunt the lion. Sometimes the lion eats us.

And underneath all these things that make us different and all these things that make us the same, there is an essence of what it means to be a human being alive on this planet. You are both unique and universal. As a human being, you can use your essential uniqueness to create something truly original and worthy of you. And you can use your essential universality to make that something truly meaningful to others.

When I hear the mockingbird sing, I'm quite aware that he is not singing to me. But I go to the window and listen because his song affects me in a unique way, just as your unique song will affect me when you share it with me.

Where we can be different from all the rest of the people around us is in the song we *choose* to sing.

WHICH SONG ARE YOU
GOING TO SING TODAY?

WHAT IS RADICAL SELF-AWARENESS?

The mockingbird isn't aware of what song he sings. Most of the time, neither are we. Radical self-awareness is the practice of noticing the songs we sing, identifying the ones that lift us up and the ones that hold us down, and understanding that we have the power—indeed, the responsibility—to choose our tune.

I have a song I sing to myself that's titled "Nothing Ever Works Out." I've been singing it to myself since I was a small child, and it's based in a story I have where I can't get what I want, no matter how hard I try. Of course, what I want is to be worthy of love. You probably have songs just like that, with your own special flavor of disappointment and resignation. We don't need others to tell us that we'll never be any good; we've already got that song down.

I have other songs, though, that lift me up, that give my heart wings, that tell me to keep flying, to keep believing that my dreams can come true. There are probably not as many of those tunes as there are ones that bring me down, but I have them. And all the love and success and growth in my life have come from my access to those songs.

RADICAL SELF-AWARENESS IS KNOWING THAT WE HAVE THE CHOICE TO CHANGE WHO WE ARE BEING.

Radical self-awareness is, as far as we know, uniquely human. It is the awareness that we have a choice in who we are being. The songbird doesn't have that choice and doesn't need it. But we do. The essential quality of every human being is the ability to own our choices.

BUILDING THE PRACTICE OF SELF-AWARENESS

If you meet someone and want to get to know them, you ask them questions. It's no different when you want to get to know yourself more deeply. In many ways, we are strangers to ourselves. When we realize this, it helps to ask a few questions to get to know ourselves better. This is how we get closer to our essence and, therefore, connect better to others.

At the heart of the Being Essential practice are seven questions. They are designed to help you develop radical self-awareness, to locate yourself on your journey, to identify who you're being and why, and to change your song when you find yourself off key.

The seven questions are simple and easy to remember. We'll spend much of this book exploring them more deeply and practicing how we can apply them to our lives and our leadership, both personal and professional.

Where are you?

The first question is about locating yourself in the moment. Where you are physically may be important, but the question really points to your state of mind. Where are you in your head and in your heart? Where are you on the journey of your years?

Why are you here?

Knowing how you arrived in this position helps you understand the situation better. Asking why you're here is nonjudgmental. You may be right where you want to be or you may be in the middle of a big mess. All that matters is recognizing the cause. Just as important, now that you're here, what does this moment ask of you? What are you called to give?

Who are you being?

When you know where you are and why, you can open the door to the question at the heart of matters. *Who are you being?* is the core question because once you know who you're being and why, you have an existential choice. You can choose to change who you are being.

What do you want?

This question is the pivot point. We spend our lives, most of us, chasing after the wrong things, things we think we want but that never satisfy us. Finally identifying what you really want, what would most make life worth living, is the essence of this work.

What wants to happen?

Is what you want aligned with the reality of the world around you? Asking *What wants to happen?* lets you survey the territory ahead of you. You may want to change, but can the world support you in that change at this time? This question deals with synchronicity and being intensely curious about what door is about to open for you.

What don't you know?

Whenever you're exploring new territory, you want to minimize the unknowns. Asking *What don't I know?* opens your mind to an examination of things to watch for and anticipate. Just as important, it's a warning to avoid the trap of knowing, which makes it impossible for us to learn or grow.

How does this feel?

The final touchpoint is a kinesthetic test. If you dismantled a figment of your self-concept that was causing you discomfort, do you feel better now? How you feel—mentally, emotionally, and physically—is your cognitive dashboard. It leads to a little question off to the side: If it doesn't feel right, then where are you? Go back to the beginning and work through the questions again and keep working until it feels right.

WHY WE NEVER RUN OUT OF QUESTIONS

It is the nature of the human mind to ask questions. It is not the nature of our minds to ask the right questions, though, nor is it in our nature to provide ourselves with authentic answers. Nor, even if we did, to pay them much attention.

Think of your neighborhood conspiracy theorists. Their minds are exploding with questions, but the questions are often based on false premises, and the answers they provide themselves—or which are provided to them on social media—make sense only in the context of those false premises. I can ask a million questions around my childish premise that nothing ever works out for me, and all my answers will be in the context of that falsehood.

But when I ask myself seven authentic questions, it helps me break the cycle of my nonsense ideas about myself. It helps me identify which voices in my head are inauthentic and not worth listening to and which voices are calling me to a real sense of who I am and what I need.

These seven questions make up an infinite flow that can

move in any direction and start at any point. So, don't think of this practice like *Give me a couple of minutes while I work through the seven questions I found in a book.* Think of it as having seven lenses through which you can see who you're being. Often, you'll get the reset you need with a single question. And soon, the questions become automatic.

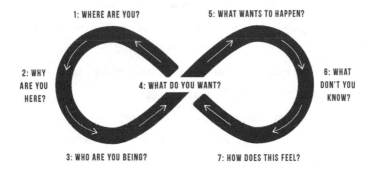

1: WHERE ARE YOU?   5: WHAT WANTS TO HAPPEN?

2: WHY ARE YOU HERE?   4: WHAT DO YOU WANT?   6: WHAT DON'T YOU KNOW?

3: WHO ARE YOU BEING?   7: HOW DOES THIS FEEL?

While there's a logic to the order and flow of the seven questions, they work equally well in reverse order. In fact, they work in any order. The practice is not linear. Asking *How does this feel?* becomes a touchstone. Listening carefully, asking the right questions, listening more, and then asking yourself how it feels is the foundation of mastery. The more practiced you become at running yourself through the seven questions, the more effective you'll be in your work, in your life, and in your relationships, including, most important, your relationship with yourself.

Imagine a dancer learning a routine. At first she has to count and learn each step and each body movement, starting and stopping and trying again. But on the night of the performance, she flows with the music and never has to think about the steps. She is entirely aware of where she is and who she is being in the moment.

Imagine if you could dance the moments of your life with that level of innate awareness of where you are and who you are being at any moment, on any day.

With practice, you will rewire your brain. Not just your mind, but the neural pathways in your physical brain. And as you do that, change takes hold in your mind and reshapes the way you think and the way you act.

We all have different ways of learning. Some of us learn from words and some from images. But all of us learn from stories. Joseph Campbell, author of *The Hero with a Thousand Faces*, explained that each of us is on a hero's journey and that each of our journeys follows a similar construction, a design framework within which we seek to understand who we are. Of course, each journey—each story—is dressed in different props and scenery. One person's may be set in the world of private jets and yachts in Monaco. Another's set on dusty desert pathways that are walked in bare feet. But those are just the externals. It's the internal journey that makes us each who we are.

This book pulls from movies and literature to illustrate learning points. It pulls from stories told by philosophers and poets. It pulls from history and religion, from Judaic,

Christian, and Islamic tales, from Hindu and Buddhist lessons, from archetypical myths from many cultures. Along the way, you'll learn from neuroscientists about how we understand the workings of the mysterious phenomenon we call *the mind*. The source of the stories isn't important. In fact, the diversity of our examples reminds us that Being Essential is, fundamentally, what unites us as humans on our unique journeys, across cultures and disciplines. We are truth seekers. It has always been this way. What's important is how your mind uses the stories to reconstruct the world you've created so you can see yourself from a new angle.

> **One can choose to go back toward safety or forward toward growth. Growth must be chosen again and again; fear must be overcome again and again.**
>
> **—ABRAHAM MASLOW**

IMAGINE YOU BEING ESSENTIAL

Go back to that mockingbird, leaping from the highest branch of the tree, celebrating his life in song. Imagine yourself having that sense of joy in being yourself. Imagine others coming to their windows to feel what you seem to be feeling.

Imagine them, through exposure to your Essential Self, finding what is essential in their own being.

Imagine forming a circle of radically self-aware leaders who are all interacting across their organizations and their communities. Imagine, as they grow, what happens to you in return. Helping others change something in themselves changes something in you.

That's the work ahead of you in this book. Go for it, as if everything depended on you Being Essential. Because everything does.

Everything depends on the individual human being, regardless of how small a number of like-minded people there are, and everything depends on each person, through action and not mere words, creatively making the meaning of life a reality in his or her own being.

—VICTOR FRANKL

THE SEARCH
for the
ESSENTIAL SELF

We have a self and a self-concept. We
live in the concept we make up.

—FRANK ALLEN

IN *THE SWITCH*, ELMORE LEONARD'S 1978 novel (later made
into the 2013 movie *Life of Crime* with Jennifer Aniston,
Yasiin Bey, and Tim Robbins), Mickey Dawson is asking
herself a series of questions. She's a wife and mother in her
mid-thirties, and she's wondering who she is and whether
she's happy. *Why do I play games with him?* she asks herself.
*Why am I afraid to tell him what I feel? Why don't I cut through
all the words and get to the point? Why am I so goddamn* nice
all the time?

She doesn't know the answers to any of these questions,

and for the first time in her life, it bothers her. At its core, the novel is Mickey's journey to find out who she is. In the beginning, she's wrapped up in a concept of herself as a mother, as a wife, as a "nice person" who is well respected at the country club in a swanky suburb of Detroit. At the end of the novel, after being kidnapped and held for ransom; after learning her husband, who has secretly filed for divorce and is in the Bahamas with his girlfriend, has decided not to pay the ransom; after escaping from the kidnappers and then befriending one of them, she finally comes to understand who she is and what she wants. It's not the escape from the kidnappers that matters in this story; that's just a metaphor for a grander, wilder escape. The heart of the story is Mickey's escape from her self-concept—the one she's spent her life letting other people construct for her—and finding her Essential Self.

To drive the point home even more clearly, Elmore Leonard uses masks as a big part of the story. The kidnappers have long conversations about the kind of masks they'll wear and the kind of mask they'll make Mickey wear when she's their captive, with the eye holes taped over so that she can't see their faces. That the masks help everyone hide their true identities is a delicious plot device. Mickey's been wearing a mask all her life, hiding who she is even from herself. At the end of the book, when she puts a mask on as a joke, as a conscious choice, it's because she's finally able to try on other ways of being.

Mickey's story is a journey toward radical self-awareness.

Her reward is to find a deeper, truer, more authentic self. That self turns out to be the voice inside her that started asking the questions and shaking the foundations on which she had built her life. Some traditions call this voice "the witness," "the inner voice," or "the conscience."

I call it the *Essential Self.*

> **Counter to what is habitual, one must find the inner, deeper self that belongs to each person who is alive in the world.**
>
> **—MARTIN BUBER**

Think about a time when you were in a state of emotional turmoil, having an angry exchange with a family member, getting upset with technology, throwing something across the room. Right in the middle of all the drama, you were probably aware of a voice in your head noticing everything that was happening and saying, *Look at you; you're really losing it.* That lone voice wasn't upset. It might have even been laughing at you, with love.

That voice is your Essential Self. Everything else roiling around in your mind is just stuff you make up, a construction of who you are, built on input from your parents, your peers, your society, and your own ego. It's built on stories you tell yourself, ideas you misunderstand, and assumptions you make. It's built on stories others tell you about yourself and identities that they give you—identities based on things like gender roles, class, race, body shape. All these stories and identities shape themselves into a self-concept. When you try to understand who you are from the point of view of your self-concept, all you can understand is the false concept. It's simply a construction.

Until you can step out of that construction, you live your life as a victim of it, missing the fullness of who you can be. Finding your Essential Self and leading with radical self-awareness is what you were born to do. It's why you are reading these words. And everything that follows is based on you getting this one idea: your life has been, and will continue to be, lived behind masks of your own making. This will be your identity until you decide to look behind the mask and find out who is really there.

YOU ARE MORE THAN THE STORIES YOU TELL YOURSELF

In their book *Changing Minds: A Journey to Awakening*, psychologists Frank Allen and Kathleen Allen-Weber write about the idea of recognizing where your mind lies. "What if we discovered," they write, "that the real problem we face is nothing more than our limited ideas about who we believe we are, our mistaken notions based on what we think is happening in this world? . . . We do not understand that our problems are created by what we think, by how we interpret what happens in our lives. Without even a modicum of genuine *Awareness*, all our attempts at problem-solving are doomed."

Self-awareness is different from self-consciousness, at least in the way our language uses the terms. Self-consciousness is the worry that others are judging us. Self-awareness is not about judgment, but about recognition. It's about identification of thoughts and of their source, not judging the thought, just noting that you're having it and noting its source. Say a person has been invited to a party where she's a fish out of water. She might sense that she feels out of place and, in a moment of self-awareness, identifies the thought as "not helpful." While she may appear out of place in this particular crowd, she recognizes that the judgment is all on her side. It is a thought that has been generated by a fearful part of her mind. She can learn to separate those fearful thoughts from her self.

That's not me, she notices. *That's just stuff I make up.*

With practice she learns to let go of judgment. Where once upon a time she might have been unable to control the negative emotion of feeling judged—or worse, might have created an experience of being judged by projecting her thoughts on others around her—she now shakes it off.

As we walk through our lives, our experience is built upon two foundations: one external and one internal. The exterior foundation of our experience is based on things that are outside our control: the weather, a barking dog, other people. The interior foundation of our experience is based on the meaning we assign to the external factors. This foundation is experienced entirely in our minds.

WHERE DOES YOUR MIND COME FROM?

We know an extraordinary amount about the structure, anatomy, and processes of the brain. We know how it works, which parts of it control different mental functions, and the extraordinary ways the hardware and software of the brain control our bodies.

But we know a great deal less about the mind. We know where humor comes from (the lower frontal lobes), but we don't know what makes it funny. There's not much in the available science that can explain how a quiet person in the corner can suddenly send everyone laughing with a well-placed and well-timed one-liner. We don't know where genius comes from or insight or kindness. We don't even know how to recreate stupidity in the lab, which you would think would be the easiest of human endeavors.

But we have some theories. So let's start with a short review of the neuroscience, focusing on how we create our human cognitive state.

We like to think of the eyes as our windows on the world through which we observe our experience of life. But it's a little more complicated than that. Our eyes are miraculous sensors of light and shadow, but we don't actually see *through* them. Instead, we process the optical impulses the brain harvests from the eyes, run them through a variety of processes in various areas of the brain, and then create an experience of vision that occurs inside our mind.

Think about that for a moment: everything you are seeing right now, you are seeing inside your mind. Not out there in the room, but inside. It's the same with hearing. Your brain processes signals that are harvested by your ears and creates a surround-sound auditory experience inside your mind. The same thing occurs with smell, taste, touch, or any kind of sensory experience. We experience the world inside our mind, at one remove from the external world we're experiencing. It's a remove as thin as moonlight, but it's a remove.

Apparently, what our brain creates is an excellent representation. It allows a race car driver to circle a track at incredibly high speeds, tires at the edge of adhesion, hitting each corner within millimeters of where the tires were on the last lap, and turning in lap after lap with variations in time of less than one one-hundredth of a second. That's a pretty good outward representation of the physical world inside that driver's mind. And from human to human, this ability appears to be pretty consistent.

A question that neuroscientists struggle with is how and where the brain creates the mind and how we come to experience a self within that mind. One explanation, put forward by Anthony Damasio, is that in creating the second-order representation described above, the brain uses its neurological structures not only to map the external world it is sensing but also to map the activity of the brain itself.

"Such newly minted knowledge adds important information to the evolving mental process," he writes. "Specifically, it presents within the mental process the information that the organism is the owner of the mental process. It volunteers an answer to a question never posed: To whom is this happening? The sense of a self in the act of knowing is thus created, and that forms the basis for the first-person perspective that characterizes the conscious mind."

> **Evolution of self rewards awareness, which is clearly a survival advantage.**
>
> —ANTONIO R. DAMASIO

We do know that our minds are constructed to understand the world in the form of story. What distinguishes the human mind from that of other species is our ability to conceive and share ideas about things that are not about the physical world. In his book *Sapiens: A Brief History of Humankind*, Yuval Noah Harari looks at reasons why, of the ten or more species of human that once inhabited this planet, only one remains.

"How did Homo sapiens manage to cross this critical threshold," Harari asks, "eventually founding cities comprising tens of thousands of inhabitants and empires ruling hundreds of millions? The secret was probably the appearance of fiction."

Something happened in the minds of early Homo sapiens that allowed our species to process our experience of the world in the form of stories. And stories are something we do know something about. In fact, neuroscientists like Damasio talk about the way we generate what he calls a "movie in the brain" and how our experience of that movie generates a sense of ownership.

In his book *Story Proof*, Kendall Haven reports on the neuroscience of how our minds interpret our experience of the world as story.

"Your brain has been hardwired to think, to understand, to make sense, and to remember in specific story terms and elements," he writes. According to the research, he says our minds create a *neural story net* that "turns sensory information into a story that makes sense to you." In other words, as you read this paragraph, your mind is assembling the random data coming in through your senses (the shapes and sequences of the letters, for instance) and making associations. It assembles all these associations into the story of a sentence, the story of a concept. Through these stories your mind creates an understanding of what you're reading. If I were speaking to you, your mind would do the same thing: it would assemble a story from the sounds you were hearing as well as from other input. How you see me, how you feel me, how you smell me, even random unrelated memories that pop up in your mind as we're talking all become part of the story of who you think I am and what you think I said.

According to Damasio and Haven, everything we experience is turned into a story as it takes shape in our minds. And, depending on what is already in our minds, we will rewrite that story to fit our experience. As we assemble our own internal experience of mind, we populate it with stories we synthesize from our external input. What doesn't make sense or fit within our self-created framework, we discard or edit until it feels cohesive to us.

In other words, we create a self-concept based on our secret, inner interpretation of our experience. I call it the *Synthetic Self.* In sharp contrast to the Essential Self, the Synthetic Self is nothing more than the collection of stories we tell ourselves. Like Mickey's story above, it is a self that is constructed of masks.

> You don't have to control your thoughts; you just have to stop letting them control you.
>
> —DAN MILLMAN

WHAT STORY ARE YOU TELLING YOURSELF?

My friends Jackie and Kevin Freiberg, who I mentioned earlier in the book and who invited me to coauthor *Nanovation*, talk about how important it is for us to get in touch with not only *what* we think but *how* we think.

"There's a phrase Jackie and I have been using whenever we find ourselves in conflict," Kevin told me. "The phrase is, '*The story I'm telling myself is . . .*' It's become a powerful tool in helping us tell each other 'where we are now' without casting judgment or blame."

I was working recently with a new CEO charged with the turnaround of a fast-growing but challenged company. Because I had coached him at his previous company, we had a strong relationship and knew each other well. As I started to work with him and his leadership team, I could feel the pressure he was under, even though he'd put the company back in the black after just one quarter, and noticed he was responding to the tension in unhealthy ways.

When he commented that if the job didn't work out, he would be sleeping under a bridge, I called a time out.

"Is that true?" I asked. "Or is that just a story you're telling yourself?" We reviewed some of the other stories he was telling himself and he started laughing. He realized it wasn't him talking; it was one of the self-judging voices in his mind.

Separating ourselves from our stories is a critical first step in locating our Essential Self. It means understanding that there's a big difference between who you are and what you make up about who you are. But there's the wonderful thing about the function of stories in the human mind: you have the power to rewrite your stories, and even to turn them off. Behind your stories, there is an Essential Self waiting for your attention, waiting to be the star of your tale.

So put the masks away, and let's take a closer look at who you really are.

THE PRACTICE

of

RADICAL SELF-AWARENESS

The world will ask you who you are, and if
you do not know, the world will tell you.

—CARL JUNG

RADICAL SELF-AWARENESS OFFERS US TWO important opportu-
nities. The first is that we can be mindful of our thoughts
and emotions; we can know where our mind is and what
stories we are telling ourselves. The second is that we can
regulate our thoughts. We can change the way we think—
not just what we think, but *how* we think. We can use it to
improve our thinking, our performance, and our experience
of life.

The scientific term for the idea that we can think about
the fact that we are thinking is *metacognition*. The idea that

we can think and, while thinking, be aware that we are thinking and, on top of that, be aware of our own awareness has fascinated philosophers and scientists since Aristotle and Buddha, and probably earlier.

My friend and fellow Reservoir colleague, Dr. Mark Lipton, has spent years studying the minds of CEOs and entrepreneurs. In an article he coauthored for *Deloitte Insights*, Lipton talks about how the most effective leaders use metacognition to improve their emotional fortitude in the face of stressful situations.

"Decision makers need to develop a clear understanding of what their emotions around a decision are and whether those emotions are appropriate," he and his coauthors write. "In other words, they cultivate great self-awareness—they practice metacognition."

RADICAL SELF-AWARENESS IS THE CORE OF BEING ESSENTIAL. WITHOUT IT, WE'RE SIMPLY AT THE MERCY OF OUR EGOS, GENERATING NEGATIVE EMOTIONS AND DOUBTS AND RESPONDING IN FEAR AND RAGE.

Metacognition is a human superpower. To explain the power of changing our thoughts, Lipton points to elite athletes as an example of how champions use radical self-awareness to regulate their attention, using it to overcome stressors and enhance performance. They know that their mindset can change, based on both internal and external input, and that their performance depends largely on their ability to recognize and adjust their mindset in the moment. At the elite level, physical performance between athletes is often well matched. What makes the difference on any given day will be the mindsets of the athletes going into the game or race. That thin tenth of a second to finish first in a race doesn't come from the legs; it comes from the mindset.

> The superpower of metacognition
> is being keenly conscious of the
> thoughts, intuitions, and feelings that
> arise when one faces a challenge.
>
> —MARK LIPTON

It doesn't matter if you're running a race or running a company. Radical self-awareness is the critical performance enhancer. It works in any field of human performance, and nowhere is it more important than in the field of leadership. And this isn't simply theoretical: mindset is such a powerful force that it actually shows up in brain scans.

Dr. Amber Selking worked closely with athletes on the University of Notre Dame football team to study how thinking differently leads to various performance outcomes. She identifies mindsets as patterned ways of thinking. You can see this through research on the brain using MRIs. Brains that are operating with debilitating mindsets have dark spots of low energy. Brains with facilitating mindsets (positive mindsets that create an optimally functioning mind) are fully lit up on the MRI. Our thoughts create mindsets and our mindsets create patterns. These patterns become hardwired into the structure of our brains and neural pathways and reconnect themselves to speed the work of the pattern.

Your mindset patterns can facilitate or debilitate your performance. Not just on the playing field but in every aspect of your life. The choice of which mindset you nurture is yours. You decide which mindset to put on when you wake up in the middle of the night, when you get out of bed in the morning, as you move through each moment of your day. Your deepest self can be brought out with positive mindsets. It can be hidden and suppressed with negative mindsets. It's your choice. You can choose to grow and exceed your perceived limitations or you can choose to scramble in the sandbox of your frustrations and fears.

CHANGE YOUR MIND, CHANGE THE WORLD

Modern science on the mind's workings, beginning with Freud, tended to focus on what was wrong with us and what was seen to be abnormal. It focused on how to fix what wasn't working. It blamed unhappiness and dysfunction on environment and other external forces. And then, in the late 1960s something happened. New voices in psychology, some influenced by the most ancient texts, began to shift the conversation from the power of the environment on our mental and emotional state to the power of our internal thinking about ourselves and the world we live in.

In 1990, Martin Seligman published *Learned Optimism: How to Change Your Mind and Your Life*, in which he showed that we have a choice in how our minds work. We can learn to be optimistic, to make positive choices, to have control over negative thinking, to change the ways we grew up thinking to achieve healthier and more productive psychological frameworks.

We have the ability, as Frank Allen said, to change minds. To switch from the negative mind of the Synthetic Self to the appreciative mind of the Essential Self as easily as switching between operating systems. So, if we have that ability, why do so few of us use it?

Seligman's work focused on the dramatically different outcomes between the pessimistic mindset and the optimistic mindset. "The defining characteristics of pessimists is that they tend to believe bad events will last a long time, will undermine everything they do, and are their own fault," he wrote in *Learned Optimism*. "The optimists, who are confronted with the same hard knocks of this world, think about misfortune in the opposite way. They tend to believe defeat is just a temporary setback, that its causes are confined to just this one case. The optimists believe defeat is not their fault."

Citing hundreds of studies, Seligman showed that pessimists have worse outcomes in every aspect of life, from relationships to careers to health. For optimists, it's just the opposite. They are far and away more likely to succeed in anything they try. His work is a fulfillment of the old saying: Optimists believe this is the best of all possible worlds; pessimists fear this is true.

In tests with incoming freshmen at the University of Pennsylvania, Seligman and his team sent the students a letter asking them to fill out a questionnaire. The questions were designed to identify those with pessimistic mindsets. Those with the most pessimistic responses were placed into a control group or invited to attend a learned optimism workshop when they arrived. Although the workshop lasted only sixteen hours, the results were profound. Over the next year, 44 percent of the control group, which had not taken the workshop, experienced periods of moderate to severe depression. Those who attended the workshop? Only 22 percent had incidents of depression; incidents were cut in half. Years later, in a similar test of cancer patients, those who received cognitive therapy designed to help them recognize pessimistic or negative thoughts had dramatic spikes in their natural immune system responses, while the control group had none.

Radical self-awareness may not cure cancer, but the science shows that it improves the outcomes of the therapy.

Dr. Tasha Eurich is an organizational psychologist who has done extensive research on self-awareness and found results that paralleled Seligman's findings on optimism. Beginning in 2014, she led a research project of ten independent studies of almost 5,000 people, one of the first of its kind. The results were startling and informative.

The participants with the highest level of self-awareness had higher job satisfaction, better relationships, and increased social and personal control, along with reduced stress, lower anxiety, and less frequent depression. They also found that self-awareness was relatively uncommon. Of the thousands of people they surveyed, many believed they had high levels of self-awareness. But the study showed that only about 15 percent of the individuals fit the criteria of being self-aware.

Interestingly, Eurich and her research team identified two types of self-awareness: internal and external. Writing in the *Harvard Business Review* in 2018, she noted, "Internal self-awareness represents how clearly we see our own values, passions, aspirations, fit with our environment, reactions (including thoughts, feelings, behaviors, strengths, and weaknesses), and impact on others. We've found that internal self-awareness is associated with higher job and relationship satisfaction, personal and social control, and happiness; it is negatively related to anxiety, stress, and depression."

External self-awareness, on the other hand, is the ability to understand how others view us and how we make them feel. "People who know how others see them are more skilled at showing empathy and taking others' perspectives," she wrote. "For leaders who see themselves as their employees do, their employees tend to have a better relationship with them, feel more satisfied with them, and see them as more effective in general."

Your mindset depends on which self you allow to write the story of your life. Will it be the self you constructed, the self you let others construct with you, the self that is made of the masks you try on to hide your feelings?

Or will it be the Essential Self, which is always there inside you, waiting for you to finally pay it some attention?

Abraham Maslow, working in the 1940s, was one of the first psychologists to move away from the study of the human being at its worst and to focus on the higher side of human potential. In his work, he identified "peak experiences as acute identity experiences." He noted that when we go through a peak experience, we feel lucky, graced, and indomitable. And yet, we also feel fearful, weak, and unworthy.

Our work here is to shed the fear and the sense of unworthiness by identifying it and switching our mindset back to the "acute identity experience," the moment when we encounter our most evolved human self, our Essential Self.

This is a subtle truth.
Whatever you love, you are.

—RUMI

An example of the conflict between the Essential and Synthetic Selves comes from playwright and author V (formerly known as Eve Ensler). In her book *The Apology*, V takes a harrowing journey inside the mind of her father, who is no longer living and who spent years abusing her sexually, physically, and emotionally. The text is a letter of apology from beyond the grave, as V goes deep inside her own self to imagine her childhood from her father's point of view.

In his story, her father describes the way he successfully hid his sense of weakness and worthlessness, his fear of being found out to be a fraud, beneath a veneer he adopted from the movie stars he saw on screen, explaining,

> The tortured and angry young man inside me was now firmly disguised, costumed in dashing handmade suits. He dressed in confidence and elegance and seemed, at least momentarily, to transform his enemies into admirers through style and charm. As you can imagine, this was a most synthetic remedy to what I can only identify now as soul sickness. I had been cast into the world as the exact opposite of the deep, reflective, philosophical man I had once dreamed of becoming. Instead, I was becoming everything I secretly despised.

Soul sickness is a vivid turn of phrase to describe the condition of trying to hide from ourselves, trying to disguise our fear and unworthiness so we will not be judged. And who will judge us more harshly than ourselves?

As V describes, the Synthetic Self is a constructed self-concept we create to hide ourselves from ourselves. Synthetic, in that we synthesize a world of our ego's own creation by assembling self-crafted bits of artificial reality and invented story. Synthetic, in that it feels indelibly real and genuine until we begin to examine it through the viewpoint of our Essential Self.

Here is your goal at the core of Being Essential and the practice of radical self-awareness: You don't have to let your Synthetic Self hog the driver's seat. You can stick that little self in the back seat and put your Essential Self behind the wheel.

WRESTLING WITH YOUR SYNTHETIC SELF

We might phrase this struggle in the language of a wrestling match because, to the Synthetic Self, that's what it is. The human ego depends on the self-concept—the Synthetic Self—you've spent your life creating. Anything that threatens the stability of that concept is terrifying. In contrast, the Essential Self isn't threatened at all. It's stable, observant, and complete. It's not self-invented. It is the essence of who you are in your deepest sense.

But that is not the self we experience most of the time

in our lives. What we experience as self is really a chattering mind that we struggle to hold in check.

In the ninth century, Junaid al Baghdadi was a renowned Sufi master. One day, he was talking to a disciple about the idea of mastery, the idea of who is in charge of the mind.

"Look at that man with the cow," he said, pointing to a farmer walking through the marketplace in Baghdad. "Who is running the show there?"

The disciple took a moment to think about it and then he said, "The farmer. He has the cow bound with a rope. The cow has to follow him wherever he goes. So obviously, he is the master."

"Really?" Junaid walked over to the farmer, who recognized the famous teacher and was honored to have his attention. "May I show my disciple something?" he said to the farmer.

Junaid took out a small knife and cut the rope, upon which the cow immediately bolted away. As the angry farmer ran after the cow, Junaid turned to the student.

"Now who is running the show?"

Junaid's lesson is about the mind. We misidentify the chattering activity of the mind as our self and think the thoughts running around our internal experience represent who we are. We think we are leading our mind through the marketplace of life, fully in control of our assets. But one slip of the rope reveals how little control we have. Like the cow in Junaid's tale, the mind has a mind of its own.

So how do we separate ourselves from our identification with all the thoughts swimming around in our heads?

COACHING THE ESSENTIAL SELF

This book is a self-coaching framework to help you guide yourself (and others) in finding solutions to issues of life, love, and leadership through radical self-awareness. Now, as you read that sentence, there are a number of reactions you might have. Take a moment to think about how you are feeling.

Are you excited and energized? Or are you feeling daunted by the effort to understand the concept? It's natural to want to avoid dealing with the Synthetic Self. It is the foundation of your personality and it has spent your whole life fortifying itself. Right now, it's probably already arguing with what you are reading. Maybe it's pointing out that this is about soft skills and doesn't focus on the serious leadership issues, like getting other people to do what you say.

I talked about this with Eric McNulty, another coach affiliated with Reservoir. Eric runs a number of leadership programs at Harvard and is the coauthor of several leadership books. He told me about a client company where people regard coaching not as a benefit but as a strike against them. They believe that you don't get offered coaching because anyone thinks it will make you better;

you get offered coaching because they think you're hopeless and likely to fail.

"Why," Eric wanted to know, "do the same people who marvel at Tiger Woods on Sunday avoid a coach for themselves on Monday?" In the world of major league sports, even coaches know they need coaches. But in our daily lives, normal people like you and me aren't always so sure we want to know what's going on in our own minds.

One reason people fear coaching is that admitting we need help is seen as a sign of weakness. Our fear of weakness is a fundamental human condition. Our first impressions of the world around us begin with the sense that the people hovering over our crib are gigantic. They're capable. They can talk and do things and make things happen. We, as infants, are completely unlike them. We look up at them and think, *They're big and I'm small. I can't do any of the things they can do. And—oh no!—I just pooped my pants again.* Everything we construct about who we believe we are is framed, in part, by that early experience of being less than.

If we are able, we learn to shed that sense of less than or, at least, understand that it's a normal part of human growth. In time, we can learn to laugh at it: *Look, there's Little Me again, thinking I'm not worthy!* But often, we can't let it go. We try to hide it with arrogance and anger, or we sink into it with chronic self-doubt and feelings of worthlessness, constantly selling ourselves short.

> The story of the human race is the story of men and women selling themselves short.
>
> —ABRAHAM MASLOW

As adults, we try to cope by hiding our sense of incompetence. So, if we ask for or accept coaching, wouldn't that be seen as an admission that we are less than? An admission that we don't know what we're doing?

That's a normal and understandable fear. But there's a deeper, more fundamental fear around the idea of coaching that's separate from the perception that it indicates weakness, and that's the fear that through coaching, we must come face-to-face with something potentially terrifying: our real self. It's our fear of what's beneath our self-concept that drives our lifelong construction project. But what lies buried beneath the construction isn't scary at all. It's rich and wonderful. That's the real self that so many of us are afraid to encounter.

So, what are you going to do with this knowledge?

Here's what the essayist Anne Lamott says: "Your problem is how you are going to spend this one odd and precious life you have been issued. Whether you're going to spend it trying to look good and creating the illusion that you have power over people and circumstances, or whether you are going to taste it, enjoy it, and find out the truth about who you are."

Here's the thing: you can start the company, build the organization, reach the top, and have it all—and it won't be enough. There's no place sadder than the silence inside the private jet and the leader who sees that having won all the prizes doesn't make any difference to how they feel about themselves. To reach the top and realize that you still don't feel good about who you are is a painful moment.

When I work with a leader in that position, we don't work on getting their stock price up or making sure their product line is positioned correctly for the coming season. And we don't work on getting them renown as a thought leader. We work on who they are being when they're sitting at their desk or walking down the hallway at headquarters. It's not that the other things aren't important; it's that leadership depends on rising above the battlefield to see what matters most.

And what matters most is knowing who you are and what you want. What matters most is making the connection to your Essential Self, so you can rise above your current circumstances to create a life that's bigger than money, power, or fame.

Nelson Mandela did that from a prison cell. Anjezë Gonxhe Bojaxhiu did that from the gutters of Calcutta. (You know her as Mother Teresa.) And you can do it from wherever you are in your life right now.

Yesterday I was clever, so I wanted
to change the world. Today I am
wise, so I am changing myself.

—RUMI

This is your moment to rise above and to see the possibilities of your life from a new perspective. What you can
see of the world from the window of that private jet can
open up your mind to wider horizons, but the view from the
last seat in the crowded coach cabin is exactly the same. And
so are the possibilities.

The person whose life is capped at tangible, synthetic
aspirations can only go so far. I've stood behind many of
them as they addressed their people at company meetings.
Most of them, and their words, will be quickly forgotten.

Essentiality is the ability to know, and to lead, what
matters most. To do that, you need to begin the work to
find and connect with your Essential Self and to practice
the kind of radical self-awareness that will transform your
experience and the experiences of those you lead.

Our practice centers on the seven questions in the pages
ahead. But first, you need to reconnect with someone inside
you who has something you need to remember, a child
inside who wants you to come out and play.

EMBRACING
your
ESSENTIAL CHILD

What did you do as a child that created
timelessness, that made you forget time?
There lies the myth to live by.

—JOSEPH CAMPBELL

WHEN I WAS A CHILD of eight, I climbed a wooden jungle gym
my father had assembled in our backyard to watch the sunset. We lived on a suburban street in California's Orange
County, a street that curved up a long slope at the start of
the foothills. The yard behind our tract house looked out
over the avocado orchards, and I could see all the way to the
orange beach ball of the sun on the horizon, the rooftops to
the west silhouetted against the sky.

That evening, I was on a mission. I was going to look

at that sunset like I'd never looked at a sunset before. I was going to memorize every single moment of it. Earlier in the day, an older woman had been visiting my parents, maybe a distant aunt of my mother's. She had said to me, "Oh, you're so lucky to have young eyes. You'll never see anything as well as you see right now."

I took this as very bad news, that my future was doomed to be duller and less beautiful, which was why I was on a mission to experience that evening's sunset in a way that I would never forget. If I was never going to see a sunset as good as that one, I needed to bank it for future reference.

That moment stuck with me and had particular resonance a few years ago when I was reading Michael Ray's book on creative thinking, *The Highest Goal: The Secret That Sustains You in Every Moment*. Since the late 1970s, Ray has been teaching a course called Personal Creativity in Business at Stanford's Graduate School of Business, a course that has become legendary, not only for the roster of incredibly famous Silicon Valley legends and business writers who took it when they were in school.

In his work, he shares about his research into a defining experience that happens to all of us early in life, an experience of what he calls our "highest goal."

"We each have an experience that we are great, that we have a connection with everything, that we have potential. This experience, if we accept it and remember it, can catapult us beyond the socialization and comparisons that deter us from living the purpose of our lives. This experience, this earliest awareness of the highest goal, can be the starting point for living with a conscious connection to it."

Ray's stories about other people's moments of experiencing their highest goals resonated deeply with me. I shot back to the moment on the jungle gym, trying to see the sunset in a way I would never forget. I think it was the experience of being totally present in the moment, my mind entirely quiet, a sense of myself as whole and complete as a human being, that is why I remembered it so clearly. And, suddenly, all those years later, I had a realization.

There's a photo of me taken at the beginning of third grade, only days or weeks after that sunset, that's unlike any other picture of me from my childhood. In it, I'm looking at the camera with a thousand-yard stare of self-knowledge and awareness, a look I always wondered about.

Now I know where it came from.

I call this memory the *Essential Child* and it's been part of my executive coaching practice for years. More than that, it defines my own best work, which is to see the world most fully as it really is, to record it in words and images, and to help others see it for themselves.

Even as you're reading this, you may be remembering your own moment (or moments, as you probably have more than one). Take a moment to write it down. We'll come back to it later.

My wife, Jean, has an Essential Child moment similar to mine. She was nine, a navy brat living in military housing outside Middletown, Rhode Island. One morning, she woke in her upstairs bedroom before the dawn. Her window was open and she felt the springtime breeze outdoors. She rose and dressed and walked outside to a place down the block where the street dropped away to the east, with a view of the dawn beginning to color the sky over the Atlantic Ocean. There was an apple tree that she had played in before, and she climbed it to look out at the ocean, feel the air moving, and watch the sunrise.

"I owned the apple tree," she remembers. "I was the master of it. It was a moment of pure contentment and essence. It was nirvana. It was, *Oh, this is perfection. This is me.*" It was an experience of her full power and completeness as a human being, her connection to the world around her, and her ability to communicate that world to others. She went on to become a CEO speechwriter, a screenwriter, a poet, and a dancer/choreographer, still fully in command of her tree.

One of my clients, a transportation executive, recalls a moment at age seven when he was riding his bike up a narrow city street in Mexico. The street was steep and he had to stand and pump the pedals, riding from side to side to lessen the grade. As he rode, he was singing at the top of his lungs. It's a moment he recalls as being totally powerful and invincible, unstoppable and joyful.

Another recalls a childhood moment when her family was staying at a lake house, and she slipped out in the early morning to sail a little sailboat alone across the lake. Like the boy on the bike, she felt in command and in control. She was one with the water and the wind. It was a feeling she used in her career as an improv comic and, later, as an executive coach.

Some people can source the memory as soon as I ask them to. But often, people protest that they can't think of anything good. I suggest they probably already thought of it and dismissed it as not important enough.

"I was just taking a walk in the woods," they say. "It's not a big deal." But, as they relive it, they understand that it was a big deal, and that is why they remember it.

I shared this idea with my friend Ronn Spencer, a highly respected photographer and one-time fixture in the Los Angeles radio world, who insisted he'd never had a moment like that as a kid. He grew up in a tough neighborhood in New Jersey, in what could be called a difficult family situation. (The HBO series *The Sopranos* was based, in large part, on his extended family.) But when I persisted, he said, "Let me try one story; maybe this is what you're looking for."

He remembered a day when he was fourteen and walked to school with a girlfriend. He didn't want to be in school that day, so he wore something that would get him sent home. Then, as he was heading back down the front steps of the school, the sun came out. He heard a noise and turned; it was the girlfriend waving to him from a third-floor window. He turned and saw a flower bed bursting with colorful spring flowers. In that moment, he experienced the profound feeling of living in a beautiful and perfect world, at which he was the center. It's interesting that, along with his work as a rock photographer, he is also known for lyrical photographs of blurred bodies, spinning gleefully in brightly colored slips, like flowers dancing in the wind.

WHY DOES YOUR ESSENTIAL CHILD MATTER?

Many coaching paradigms begin by imagining a future state—a person we want to become—and then setting goals to work toward that future. In Being Essential, we're digging back to an existing self that is the foundation of who we are and who we are becoming.

Finding your Essential Child and bringing her forward

to your present and into your future is the core of this work. The reason you develop your Essential Self is not so that you can reach some distant goal. Being the Essential Self *is* the goal. Everything that matters flows from it, including all of your future. Disconnected from the Essential Self, future goals are child's play, made-up games in a made-up world.

Your childhood moment—and who you were being in that moment—is a foundational building block, a touchstone for any future goal you will ever contemplate. The question your Essential Child will ask you is this: Is this goal big enough for your Essential Self?

We are not so much human beings
as we are human becomings. We
spend our lives becoming all of
whom we have it within us to be.

—MARGIE WARRELL

FINDING YOUR ESSENTIAL CHILD

Often, just reading or hearing about this concept causes your Essential Child to jump up and wave at you. You remember a moment almost instantly. You may remember several. If that's the case with you, take a moment right now to write down what you remember about that experience.

- What time of day was it?
- Where were you?
- Why were you there?
- What did you see?
- What do you remember thinking and feeling?

As you write, see if the notes trigger any other memories for you. If they do, write those down too. This child is resilient. It has weathered everything you've thrown at it all your life, every mistake, every stumble, every wrong turn. It just patiently waits for you to remember it and create another moment of timelessness.

But if no memory presents itself, don't worry. It will come. Here are a few ways to coax it into the present.

Recall your first memory in life

There's a reason you remember that moment, a reason that moment stayed in your consciousness.

My first memory comes from when I was two years old, in the very spot I'm standing in this picture. In my memory, there's an older girl sitting on the steps with her baby sister. I'm holding a pencil and a piece of paper and I'm telling her that I know how to write.

"No, you don't," she says, shaking her head. "You don't know how to write."

So I hold the paper against my palm and I show her. I put the pencil to the paper. It goes straight through, and the sharp lead point sticks deep into the palm of my hand.

What I remember most about that moment is not pain, but a very specific surprise: I *knew* that I knew how to write. Every fiber of my two-year-old self knew it, like it was a memory from a distant past. In very significant ways, I have spent the rest of my life trying to prove to myself and to others that I can write. It's been at the core of my career almost all my life.

What's your first memory as a child? Start there, and then work on other memories from childhood that seem meaningful. Why are they meaningful? Why do you remember them?

Look for a moment of connection

Childhood isn't all laughs. Often, there are moments when we don't feel loved or valued. And then somebody puts a puppy in our lap. Or a horse sticks its head through a fence to sniff us and we feel a sense of belonging. Write down some of those memories.

There's a saying in Hollywood that every movie starts in one of two ways: either someone goes on a journey or a stranger comes to town. Maybe you went on a family vacation or were sent to stay with a grandmother. Look for moments of connection there.

Or maybe someone came to visit. I was four when my uncle Tony came to town. While he was there, he made me feel important and interesting in a way no other adults bothered to do. That sense of connection stayed with me for a very long time because he was the first adult who treated me as a person worth listening to.

Maybe it was a teacher who really got you. Maybe it was an elderly person who was deeply present with you. Look for any moment where you sensed a deep connection to something or someone else.

Take a meaningful moment from the present

If you can't find a childhood moment, Michael Ray suggests looking for more recent moments of meaning. "Recall the most meaningful thing you did in the last week or so," he writes. "Whatever it is, reexperience doing that activity.

See it in your mind's eye and get the feeling of what made this activity so meaningful." It doesn't have to be earth-shaking, just an event or activity that you remember as meaningful. Write down what you remember about the experience.

Then, ask yourself what about that moment was meaningful to you. What makes it feel important? Write that down so you remember it.

Next, ask yourself why it was so important. What about the answer you gave to the question above is so important to you?

Then, ask again: What was important about *that* answer? With each reason you give yourself, ask the question again: Why is *that* so important?

Keep going until you get it down to a single word. What's the one word or phrase that can help you define it? Pulling from my childhood moment watching the sunset, my word is *vision*. Yours might be *teacher* or *guide* or *trailblazer*. Whatever it is, use it to call you back to your Essential Child.

One of my coaching clients couldn't remember anything good at all from his rough upbringing, but he had mentioned how much he loved his Harley-Davidson motorcycle. I asked him to remember the day he bought his first one and rode it home.

"After you rode it home and parked it in your garage," I asked, "did you go back out to look at it later?" It turned out he had. In the quiet of his garage, with his hands on the handlebars and his feet on the ground, he felt the strength and power at the core of the machine. That was a sense of profound peace and potential for him, and it became the place we came back to in coaching, time and time again. For him, that moment called him back to a place where he had the power to take control of his life and to move forward.

Think of a moment in your life when time seemed to stand still, when everything around you seemed to be imbued with meaning.

Life is full of such moments, but sometimes we fail to notice them. So if nothing comes to mind from childhood, start looking for a moment of essentiality in your life right now. You'll find it.

WHAT IS TRUE ABOUT YOU?

My wife once asked me, "What is true about you?" As I was thinking of a reply, she answered for me: "You always find the light." In my darkest times, times when I feel most discouraged, most lost, I always find the light. The me that found that light was my Essential Child, the me that sat in a high place and looked at the light of the sun on the far horizon. The Essential Child is the foundation of the Essential Self.

These Essential Child memories bring instant clarity to radical self-awareness: either the thought or internal condition you're experiencing is consistent with your Essential Child, or it's not. You know, intuitively, when it is and when it isn't. Forget spirit guides or fairy godmothers; your Essential Child is the best guide you have.

Radical self-awareness sounds hard, even tiring, but it's not. It's like learning to dance. Once you know how, it comes easily. That doesn't mean you won't misstep, but you'll get back on the beat and keep going.

Like the girl in the tree, the boy on the bike, or the girl sailing across the lake, connect with that child as though everything in your life depends on it. Because it does. I urge you to go all in on finding the source of your Essential Self.

When we align our thoughts, emotions, and actions with the highest part of ourselves, we are filled with enthusiasm, purpose, and meaning. Life is rich and full.

—GARY ZUKAV

WHERE *are* YOU?

You've got to find yourself first.
Everything else'll follow.

—CHARLES DE LINT

GOD'S FIRST QUESTION

ON APRIL 20, 1947, THE philosopher Martin Buber gave a talk in the Netherlands. It was part of a program to reestablish the normal channels of interaction between universities and academics across Europe and other parts of the world. Buber, an Austrian Jew, had survived World War II in Israel, where he taught at the Hebrew University in Jerusalem. This was his first visit back to Europe.

He began his lecture by telling a Hasidic tale about a rabbi in St. Petersburg who has been arrested on suspicion of being, well, probably just a Jew. As the rabbi sits in his cell in meditation, he is visited by the chief of police. The chief is impressed by the rabbi's serenity. He begins a conversation with the rabbi about a question from scripture that has always intrigued him.

> The chief of police asked: "How am I to understand that God, who is omniscient, asks Adam, 'Where are you?'"
>
> The rabbi replied: "Do you believe that scripture is eternal and encompasses every age, every generation, and every person?"
>
> "Yes, I believe that," said the chief.
>
> "Well now," said the Zaddik, "in every age God addresses every person with the question, 'Where are you in your world? Already so many of your allotted years and days have passed. How far have you come

in your world?' Perhaps God will say, 'You have lived
forty-six years. Where are you now?'"

When the chief of police heard the exact number
of his years, he pulled himself together, clasped the
rabbi's shoulder, and exclaimed: "Bravo!" but his heart
trembled.

Buber spoke with a profound sense of where he and his
audience were on their journey. It was two years after World
War II and no one was unaware of what had happened to
the Jews, who had been their neighbors, friends, and colleagues before the war. Whether they had been rounded up
by the Nazis or had emigrated to North America or Israel,
they were gone. And so the Hasidic tale of the imprisoned
rabbi and his wisdom to answer the policeman's question
on an entirely different level than it was asked would have
resonated strongly.

They knew where they were as individuals: in a devas-
tated post-war Europe, in an academic world just beginning
to rebuild, their personal lives in tatters (if they were lucky).
They knew they were in a state of shock and recovery as they
tried to restore their civilization. They knew they were at the
conference because they wanted to be part of the rebuilding
process. And each, within themselves, was in a place of grief
or denial, hope or determination.

And so the reminder that "Where are you?" was God's
first question recorded in the Bible was not an idle one.
Buber knew where his audience was, and God knew where

Adam was. He knew Adam was hiding. When he asked, "Where are you?" he was asking Adam to consider his own self-awareness.

Buber explains that the rabbi did not answer the police chief's question nor did he address the text. That's not where he was. He didn't need to banter theology with his captor. "Instead," says Buber, "he departs from the text and uses it as a stepping-stone to make the chief of police search his own soul and admonish his own past life: his frivolity, his thoughtlessness, and his lack of a sense of responsibility." Instead of letting his captor judge him, the rabbi asks the chief to judge himself. Not cruelly, but with compassion and humanity, which he himself was denied.

Where was the rabbi? In his place as a spiritual teacher. And the police chief? Something drew him into the room, apart from his professional duty. Something about the rabbi's presence affected him. Whether he knew it or not, he was there to learn something about himself.

So take a moment to ask yourself this question. *Where are you?* In the years that have passed since that Essential Child awoke in you, how far have you come? Where are you now?

AWARENESS IS A DELICATE DANCE

One of the most beautiful images in movie history is the tango scene from *Scent of a Woman*. If you've seen it, you know the moment. Al Pacino plays Frank Slade, a retired US Army lieutenant colonel who is blind. When a woman, played by Gabrielle Anwar, hears a band playing tango music, she mentions that she's always wanted to learn the tango, but her boyfriend thinks it's silly. Frank offers to teach her. After asking for the layout of the dance floor, he guides her to the center, and as the band begins to play, we see a blind man leading a woman in her first tango.

The scene is beautiful because we know that Frank is a deeply lost man who has told us he may soon take his own life. But for the duration of a single song, with a woman he cannot see, on a dance floor he can only feel through the soles of his shoes, he moves with grace and conviction. Because, at that moment, he knows where he is.

When the tango is over, we know the woman's life has been transformed (and her poor boyfriend's is probably about to be). And we know that Frank's can be, too, if he can come to terms with where he is in his own personal dance, the broader and more challenging journey of his life. Will he reestablish himself as a leader? Will he rediscover his ability to transform his own life and others? Will he finally learn how to love?

By the end of the movie, Frank knows where he is. He has rejoined himself. The tango is a metaphor for the profound sense of place he arrives at in the closing scene of the film.

If we were writing a movie that began with the rabbi and the police chief meeting in the jail, it would be the beginning of the chief's journey to find himself. The rabbi is simply the instigator who issues what Joseph Campbell named *the call to adventure*. The chief would at first resist the call, arguing that he is too busy with his duties. And after all, he lives in a world where his job is to arrest old rabbis, not embark on a life-changing journey because of one. But in our movie, he would find himself irresistibly drawn to a quest. A quest to discover where he is and where he needs to go. In the end, he'll face a crisis of the soul that will propel him to the action of the finale where he either saves the day or loses the battle. Either way, he comes back to where he began, as a changed person.

Your movie is the same. Like Lt. Col. Frank Slade, you will have to dance without being able to see where you are going. And you will have to find yourself in that dance. That's the hero's journey. It's a dance with oneself, a dance to find your profound sense of place in the world.

Pay attention to your attention.

—OTTO SCHARMER

In Buber's tale, the policeman's question was a form of provocation, perhaps intended to reveal a flaw in the framework of Jewish thought. But the rabbi's response ignores the literal meaning of the question and goes straight to the chief's heart. In effect, he says to the chief, "You, yourself, are Adam; it is you whom God addresses. Where are you?" And he tells us that the chief's heart trembled at the rabbi's words.

"It is this self-awareness," Buber tells us, "that is decisive for the beginning of the *way* in a person's life."

Asking *Where am I?* is the first step in calling your attention back to your Essential Self and being fully alive in the moment. This question comes first because it helps us locate ourselves. It can be as broad as asking where you are on the journey of your years, as the rabbi asks the chief. It can be as specific as asking what room you are in. And it can be as internal as identifying the headspace you find yourself in.

This question calls you to presence.

Knowing where you are calls for awareness in every sense. Literally, every *sense*: using sight, hearing, smell, and touch to locate yourself, not just in the room where you're sitting or the chair you're sitting in, but in your own skin, in the present moment. Can you feel the air moving on your forearms or the back of your neck? Can you feel the humidity or the air pressure? When the air conditioner kicks in, can you feel it? Can you hear it? Can you detect a scent in the air? Those senses locate you and help you identify where you are.

To answer the question *Where am I?* you must tune in to everything you can sense right now. It's not about cataloging or listing the sensations you're aware of. It is simply quieting your mind enough to notice them and, having noticed, to spend a moment being with them, paying close attention.

Begin with curiosity, with the desire to locate your Essential Self within the clutter of thought impulses we call the mind. So often, we're dancing like a puppet on the strings of our thoughts without any awareness of where we are or why. We may know we're in the car, stuck in traffic. We may know we feel unhappy to be there. Or are we unhappy about something else? Who knows? We try not to think about it, but the thoughts keep coming, a random, meaningless progression.

Watch a dog sitting on a lawn in the first light of day, reading the morning breeze. Her ears are perked up and her head is cocked, listening to the sounds of dawn. Her nose is lifted, scanning slightly from side to side as she twitches the muscles of her snout, working the intricate mechanisms of scent, her strongest sense. A dog has very little sense of self or time, and almost no memories, but she's intensely aware of where she is.

That's why early humans learned to value dogs as early warning systems, because dogs pay attention to what's going on around them. In that, they are aided by what might seem to be a deficit: they can't think of the future or the past, at least not very far in either direction. You and I, however, can dwell in the past or the future, and in fact, that's where we spend most of our life on earth, either remembering or rehashing events and conversations that happened years or minutes ago or projecting our past onto our future, imagining and "pre-living" encounters we've scheduled for later in the day or later in our life.

It's not that that in itself is bad. It's our past experience of navigating our landscape in a human body that allows us to run up a flight of stairs without falling. Our past experience of negotiating interactions with other people helps us (hopefully) find the correct response to interactions with the people we meet in different situations. But if we don't know, in that interaction, that we're framing our response in terms of our past, then we may miss important information about the present moment.

Imagine you're interviewing candidates for an important leadership post on your team. As you read through the material on each person and meet with them, your mind will be feeding you lenses through which to look at them. These lenses are biases, patterns of thought and association we've been fed all our lives, patterns we've created for ourselves without ever realizing we were doing it. Those patterns may keep you from correctly assessing the talent that's right in front of you.

When, in that kind of situation, you take a moment to ask yourself where you are, you can pull yourself up to a more aware state of mind. *Oh, right,* you remind yourself, *I always look at the pattern, not the person. Let me change my lens and really see this person I'm speaking with from my Essential Self. Let me see if I can meet their Essential Self.*

True navigation begins in the human
heart. It's the most important map of all.

—ELIZABETH KAPU'UWAILANI LINDSEY

THE LEADER AS NAVIGATOR

Leadership requires presence, the ability to identify where
your mind is in the moment. And more than that, it requires
a positioning sense that allows a leader to identify coordi-
nates with which to navigate. A leader needs to be able to
identify the team's place, or the project status, or the state of
the market at any point in time and space.

Much like we use GPS to identify the position of a
vehicle or airplane, a self-aware leader identifies the position of whatever it is they are leading so that they can steer
around obstacles and toward goals. You can't plan your journey without knowing from where you begin.

Here's an example of using question one to promote
self-awareness along with a greater awareness of a team
goal in an organizational setting. On a recent project, the
Reservoir team was invited to identify ways in which one of
the world's largest and most important ports could accel-
erate the adoption of zero-emission trucks for the port's
drayage fleet. Drayage trucks haul shipping containers in
and out of the port, normally making short-haul runs of
less than 300 miles in a day. With as many as 15,000 diesel

trucks serving the port on any weekday, they present a troubling challenge to clean air efforts. At the time, the goal was to convert the entire fleet to zero-emission vehicles within fifteen years.

Where were we? It was December of 2020, the year of some of the most intense fires in the history of California, where the port is located. It was the year people learned the word *pyrocumulus* to describe clouds of fire in the sky. It was just eleven months after vast areas of Eastern Australia burned in the same terrifying way. From that vantage point, it was clear to us that the devasting effects of global warming were not in the future. Climate change was right in front of us.

So, we decided to look at what it would take to cut that zero-emission target window in half.

We started with three areas of inquiry. First, we wanted to know where the current state of drayage trucking was at the port. What were the trends, in both human and vehicle terms, that would affect the rate of change? Second, we asked where the zero-emission trucks would come from. Where were the manufacturers, in terms of being able to deliver affordable trucks in the numbers we needed? And third, we had to assess where the region's power grid was in its development cycle. Would the utilities be able to generate enough power to meet the needs of electric vehicles? Where was their development of alternative power sources so that the power used was zero emission at each step of the process?

In effect, we had to map out the territory of the present and future states. We had to know where each part of the puzzle was and where each would be year by year. And we had to know where our team was in relation to the questions we asked. Did we have the right consultants and advisors on the team? We had sixty days to deliver our report, so we had to know where we were on our timeline. Along the way, fresh insights emerged that caused us to change direction more than once.

As the project head, I had to be deeply aware of where my mind was, as well as maintain a constant awareness of where my colleagues were with their parts of the project. Two weeks before the completion date, I had a sense that we were missing something big, but couldn't locate the gap. When I went to bed, I set my mind to feed me the idea I needed when I awoke the next morning. And sure enough, when I got to my desk the following morning, I saw what we had been missing: the data that could provide us the insight on where the fleet was at any moment and AI that would allow us to maximize efficiencies in planning traffic and load distribution. The data literally connected all the parts. It showed us where everything was at any moment. It was the essential ingredient we had been missing.

The result was a plan that, if enacted, not only would get the port to the target in approximately half the previous estimate but would provide financial benefits to the thousands of drivers and small trucking companies that served the port while reducing the number of trucks needed in the fleet. It would also benefit the manufacturers by providing a revolving investment fund to help them bring their trucks to market faster. Most of all, it would remove a massive amount of air pollution from the region.

All because we started the project by asking *where*.

A leader who intends to show people the way in any organization needs to know where the organization stands at any moment. Like a dancer leading a tango, one needs the floorcraft to know where they are and where they are going. And like a rabbi sitting in a police chief's cell, a leader needs to know where they are in the moment so they can steer the conversation and the thinking of others to a new kind of clarity.

So, ask where you are and keep asking so you can develop a deeper sense of place in the world you seek to lead.

WHY

are you

HERE?

If you want heaven, start in mud. Begin
transfiguration where you're stuck.

—MARK TREDINNICK

TO ASK WHERE YOU ARE is to locate yourself in the moment. To ask why you are here gives the moment—and your leadership—meaning and direction. Imagine, for instance, that you're leading a group of students through a master class on the paintings of Caravaggio. *Why are you here?* Because, after years of work and study, you have come to be recognized as one of the leading experts on the subject. And why else are you here? Maybe it's because you are called to light a spark in the hearts of your audience, a spark that can transform how they see the world. Maybe it's even more specific; maybe you are there to help a single person have a breakthrough. Their breakthrough may depend on how focused you are on why you are here.

The power of this question is to supercharge your life and your leadership with purpose. If you are here because you are being asked to take account of past actions and decisions that have caused what feels like a wrong turn, that realization can become your turning point for change. If you are here because you are called to help someone else find their own turning point, that's a powerful reason to identify in the moment. And if you have no idea why you're here, then your purpose is to be intensely curious about what the moment asks of you.

This simple question calls you to understand your meaning in the moment.

As the poet Mark Tredinnick points out, the road to heaven begins with recognizing that you can choose to experience life not as a series of predictable events but as an opportunity to create meaning at every turn.

A MORNING AT A CROSSROADS

When I was twenty-one, I found myself standing at a crossroads in western Kansas. It was a June morning, and I was surrounded by rolling fields of wheat that stretched as far as you could see. I'd spent the night on a picnic table at a country rest stop at the corner of Interstate 70 and a county road. At sunrise, I walked out to the on-ramp and put out my thumb, hoping I could hitch a ride.

I was on my way from college in California to New York, and possibly points beyond. I had an idea that I would spend the summer visiting friends, working on my writing, and maybe studying yoga.

At the crossroads, the going was slow. The few local cars that came by sped away when they saw me. I considered walking up the ramp to see if I could flag down an eighteen-wheeler or some sympathetic longhairs in a VW van, when I saw a pickup truck exit the freeway on the other side of the road.

The driver stopped at the intersection and looked my way. Then he slowly pulled across the road and motioned for me to hop in. He was a man my father's age, in his forties. He asked where I was going and I told him New York.

He told me he was headed over to the county seat. He explained that his son had just graduated from UCLA. "He called me last night and told me he's not coming home. He's not going to help me on the farm and he's not going to take it over. So, I'm going down to the courthouse to file for bankruptcy."

I didn't know what to say, so I started asking questions, and as I did, I felt a call to be someone new. I realized I might be the one person in the man's life who could help him understand his son's decision. In that moment, I had a profound understanding of why I was there.

I remember trying to express to him what it felt like to be twenty-one years old in America, particularly in California. The sense of change and expanding possibilities that we felt, even as there were grave social challenges, culture wars, and real wars to fight. I tried to think about how such dramatic change would look to a wheat farmer in western Kansas. Where was the seed of adventure in him that I could connect to the seed blooming in his son, and in myself?

For about thirty minutes, we talked as we rode together. When we reached the outskirts of the county seat, he went down the off-ramp and pulled onto the shoulder.

"I changed my mind," he said. "I'm keeping the farm. I'll find a way to make this work."

I shook his hand and watched as he made a U-turn and headed back the way he had come, ready to give his life a second chance.

That ride was an early appearance—and the most powerful to that time—of a larger, essential version of myself that I would grow into in the years ahead. In a very real sense, I wasn't only at the crossroads to meet a farmer. I was there to meet my once and future self, my Essential Self, a person who can help other people look at where they are and why, so they can create meaning in their lives.

YOUR HERO'S JOURNEY IS TO DISCOVER
WHAT YOU NEED TO CHANGE AND WHY

In 1960, director Billy Wilder shocked American sensibili-
ties when he released *The Apartment,* a film that dealt frankly
with sexual abuse in the workplace. Part of what shocked
audiences was that it was a romantic comedy.

The film follows two workers in a Manhattan office
building as they struggle to find self-worth in their lives.
C.C. Baxter, played by Jack Lemmon, is a lowly desk jockey
with a problem: he has a small apartment near Central Park
that top executives in the company use for extramarital
affairs (usually with women who work for them), and he
often can't go home because it's so popular. Elevator oper-
ator Fran Kubelik is one of the employees being taken to
Baxter's apartment. She's fallen for Jeff Sheldrake, head of
personnel, but knows he's lying when he says he loves her
and wants to leave his wife.

Baxter gets a promotion for being so accommodating
to Sheldrake and the others and hopes that, as a rising star,
he can win the attention of Miss Kubelik. But Fran has had
enough. Not knowing whose apartment she's in—humiliated
by Sheldrake and ashamed that she's let herself be used as a
sex object—she attempts suicide with Baxter's own sleeping
pills. He finds her in time and saves her life.

As the movie enters the third act, each of them knows
that they're living miserable lives. But it's not until they
identify *why* they are where they are that they are able to
change. That discovery—asking *Why am I here?*—leads

to the character transformation at the heart of the hero's journey. Baxter quits his job and Fran quits Sheldrake. In doing so, they each find a sense of their own worth, which in time allows them to find each other.

Why were they there? Because they were letting other people use them. When they decided not to do that anymore, they were able to find their own purpose and pursue their own happiness.

The Apartment took home five Oscars, including Best Picture and Best Director for Billy Wilder, Best Actor for Jack Lemmon, and Best Actress for Shirley MacLaine. It's still one of the most praised films of the twentieth century. The film's success is based on the universality of the human problem the characters address: we know we don't like where we are, but we don't know how to change it. The story is as relevant in the twenty-first century as anything you'll see this year because almost all of us, at one time or another, are trying to escape a life that feels like a trap and are unable to do so because we haven't realized why we are here.

Did you question your story? It's not easy. For some of us, that story is a big part of our identity. We do not easily give it up.

—GREGG KRECH

The question *Why am I here?* has an important flip side, which can be worded: What am I here for? Once Baxter and Fran identified what had brought them to the third act of the movie—the part when they have to change their minds and move toward what they want most—they see everything that's happened, every frame of the film, as a call to change their stories. And, in this case, what brought each of them to their moment of realization was the call to find love and meaning in their life and to share it with each other.

In this context, we ask ourselves: What are we here to learn? What are we here to give? What part of some great cosmic puzzle are we called to solve? When you are curious enough to ask these questions, interesting things begin to happen to you and to those around you.

TALKING TO NOW: BEING PRESENT TO THE NEEDS AROUND YOU

Why am I here? That was the question Father Gregory Boyle asked himself one day in 1986, standing on the steps of the Dolores Mission in the Boyle Heights neighborhood of Los Angeles. A thirty-three-year-old Jesuit priest, he had been working as a teacher in Bolivia and had discovered that he was much more called to working with the poor than he was to teaching. As a result, his superiors sent him to Los Angeles as the youngest pastor in the history of the diocese.

Dolores Mission sits between Pico Gardens and Aliso

Village, two notorious housing projects that were the home turf of eight gangs. "If Los Angeles was the gang capital of the world," he writes in his memoir, *Tattoos on the Heart*, "our little postage-stamp-sized area on the map was the gang capital of L.A."

Father Greg's *Why am I here?* moment was simple. Most of his parishioners were women. The parishioners weren't only losing their peace of mind in all the violence; they were losing their children. He could focus on their needs, hire guards, and put up fences to protect the church. Or he could focus on what they needed most, which was to reduce the gang violence around them. Father Greg understood that he was not there simply to perform mass, hear confession, and take care of church business. He was there to help people heal themselves and their community. So, with their help, he set out to learn what the gang members wanted and how he could help them get it.

It's nice to have "big picture," "meaning of life" answers to the question of why we're here. As a Jesuit priest, Father Greg has plenty of those kind of answers. But the big picture is sustained by a lifetime of moments when you ask yourself the question, *Why am I here right now, with these people, in this situation?* Because life is not a generalized concept. Life is very specific.

WHY ARE YOU HERE?
TO GIVE WHAT THE MOMENT
ASKS OF YOU.

People say Greg Boyle has saved a lot of lives. But he's also buried so many of the young men and women he's worked with. Even when someone is trying their best to leave the past behind, it has a way of catching up with them when they least expect it. Waiting for a bus. Standing on a corner. Driving through the old neighborhood just once . . . and bullets fly. That's why Father Greg understands that he has to value the moments and understand why he's there with anyone who knocks on his door.

It is important, especially as a leader, to remember why you are here: when you are tired, and someone who is always working through emotional problems knocks on your car window as you're going home for the day; when you're trying to protect your time so you can work on a presentation, and a direct report needs ten minutes; when you have to go to a meeting, and someone in the hallway needs encouragement but is too shy to say so. These are the moments that move your story forward. They're no more or less important than the moment you open a global sales conference or close a mega deal or ring the bell at the stock exchange to take your company public. They're all part of a matrix of moments, large and small, where you take the time to understand what the specific moment is asking of you. Because, in responding to the smallest moments, a culture of right action is born.

It would be easy to say, "Well sure, Father Greg is a priest. That's what he's supposed to do. But I have an organization to run. I don't have time for people's problems."

Father Greg Boyle has an organization to run too. It's called Homeboy Industries, and over the years it's provided employment, advancement, and a chance at life for more than 15,000 gang members. You can buy coffee and a doughnut at their bakeries, including the one at Los Angeles International Airport. They have the world's largest tattoo-removal service, because it's hard to move forward in a straight career if you have the F-word tattooed on your forehead.

No, having an organization to run doesn't free you from having to understand why you're in the position you're in. It's the reason you ask this question.

Why are you here?

Every time Father Greg, tired and ready to go home, gets stopped in the parking lot by someone asking for a minute of his time, he no longer has to ask why he's here. He knows.

When you follow a star you know you
will never reach that star; rather it
will guide you to where you want to
go. So it is with the world. It will only
ever lead you back to yourself.

—JEANETTE WINTERSON

WE'RE HERE BECAUSE WE'RE HERE

Drive north from New Delhi for 100 miles, through the broad plains and fertile fields of wheat, to the town of Kurukshetra, the setting for one of the greatest philosophical discussions in history. Today, you'll see everything from trucks and buses to tuk-tuks and carts pulled by oxen down long, leafy lanes. You'll see modern office buildings representing the wealth of India's participation in the global economy, and you'll see squalid tent cities where people struggle to find their next meal. But what you won't see is one of the most famous fictional battlefields in history, for this fertile quarter of India is the setting for the *Bhagavad Gita*, one of the foundational texts of Hindu thought.

The *Gita* begins with two great armies arrayed against each other, ready to battle to the death. As the war trumpets blow, Prince Arjuna asks his charioteer, Lord Krishna, to drive to a high place where he can overlook the battleground and get a sense of what is about to happen. As he surveys the armies spread out on the plain, he sees his friends and family lined up on both sides and is horrified. It makes no sense, and he asks Krishna to tell him why he shouldn't lay down his arms and refuse to fight.

> Shall I deal death on these
> Even though they seek to slay us? Not one blow,
> O Madhusudan! will I strike to gain
> The rule of all Three Worlds; then, how much less
> To seize an earthly kingdom!

What Arjuna wants to know is simple: Why should I participate in this insanity? Why shouldn't I walk away from all this? *Why am I here?*

Lord Krishna's answer, though not short, is simple. You are here because you are here. It is your purpose to be here and also the burden you bear, your karma. And being here calls you to action, to fulfill your destiny, your *dharma*.

So why are you here, reading this chapter? The simple answer would be that you are looking for something. The deeper, richer answer—the one that speaks to life, love, and leadership—is that everything you've done in your life, every choice, every seemingly accidental turn of events, has led you to this moment, when you have the choice to move the story forward or withdraw and reverse your journey. What each of us does in each moment is a choice. Will you lead or will you walk away?

That's the question Krishna poses to Arjuna.

When we look for the meaning of life, we want a story that will explain what reality is all about and what my particular role is in the cosmic drama.

—YUVAL NOAH HARARI

Modern minds might argue that war is useless and ends badly and Arjuna could try to change the outcome of the moment. But that misses the point. The battleground of the *Gita* is not a real battleground; it is a metaphor for the struggle of life, in which we are born into a world—a playing field—where the rules often seem absurd and the results never change. In the end, we all die.

On the field of play, to ask *Why am I here?* is to investigate your purpose—not over the broad and cosmic span of your life, but in the moment in which you find yourself.

The day I stood outside my office at the tech company and realized I was fighting a battle I was destined to lose, I found myself at another crossroads moment. I could have blamed others for my failure, but I didn't. Instead, I decided to step back and take a long look at the decisions that led me to take the job in the first place, and I recognized that it was the Synthetic Self who had made those decisions.

Asking why I was there and what I needed to learn from the experience turned that failure into a launching pad for future success.

WHO
are you
BEING?

All experience happens for one purpose
only: to expand your awareness.

—PAUL FERRINI

THE MONK WHO CARRIED A WOMAN FIVE MILES

THERE IS A ZEN PARABLE about two monks on a journey. They come to the banks of a fast-moving stream in the mountains, where they find a woman who is afraid she'll be washed away if she tries to cross the water. She begs them to help her.

The monks have taken vows that are very clear: they can never touch a woman, let alone hold her in their arms. The younger monk kindly explains this to her and then begins to wade across alone.

But the older monk sweeps her up and, lifting her clear of the water, splashes across the stream, laughing joyfully. He puts her down on the opposite shore and continues on his way.

The young monk is stunned. Still standing in the middle of the stream, he can't believe what he saw. He stomps out of the water, bows hurriedly to the woman, and chases after his companion.

All the way along the five miles to their destination, the younger monk is in conflict. What should he do? The rules have clearly been broken. If he says nothing, he is complicit. His companion may care nothing for the sanctity of their vows, but the entire structure of the *dharma* depends on discipline and respect of the law. And here, his brother monk has defied the vows. In the face of wrong action, isn't right action required?

He makes the painful decision that, as much as it hurts

him to do so, when they reach the temple, he will have to report the infraction to their abbot or risk being tainted himself. But first, he feels it's only fair to share his feelings with the older monk and tell him what he plans to do.

"What were you thinking back there? You held a woman in your arms as if you had no vows at all! And in front of me! I'm still so shocked I don't know what to do, but I have to say something."

The older monk looked at him, laughed, and rubbed the young monk's cue-ball head.

"The girl? I put her down five miles ago. Why are you still carrying her?"

In this story, who is the young monk being? And what about the older one? The younger monk not only "carried the woman five miles," he carried a heavy burden of judgment as well. Who are you being when you are carrying judgments? You're in a state of self-justification. Why? Because one way not to condemn yourself is to stay busy condemning others. The young monk wasn't truly concerned with who the older monk was being or what he had done. He was battling with his own confused self, and to mask his confusion and elevate himself in his own estimation, he was judging the other. He was actually disassociated with reality because any child could have told him what to do in the situation with the woman by the stream.

Suppose the woman had fallen into the water and was calling for help as she washed downstream. Would the young monk have explained, "Hey, wish I could help, but you know the rules"? Of course not. He would have plunged in to save her. The rules would be irrelevant.

On the day he joined the order, the young monk would have known the right action because he would have been in what the Zen tradition calls "beginner's mind." In beginner's mind, you can simply act without thinking because you haven't been bound up with expertise. You think all things are possible. But in the intervening time, in his honest attempt to be a good monk, he became an expert on the rules and lost touch with what mattered most, which is at the heart of the Zen practice: *Who are you being?*

On the other hand, the older monk knew exactly who he was. He understood that the rules meant that one shouldn't touch a woman with a sexual intent. In helping her across the stream, he had no such intent. He simply did what the moment asked of him, and in doing so, he sparked joy. He knew the essence of where he was and why he was there.

Doing what's right isn't the problem. It is knowing what's right.

—PRESIDENT LYNDON BAINES JOHNSON

Author and speaker Kevin Freiberg and I have spoken about this inner dichotomy. He describes it as the difference between the truth of your being (who you really are) and the way of your being (how you act).

"*The truth of my being*," he said, "is one who is loved and accepted unconditionally, now and forever. But *the way of my being* is often harsh, judgmental, and riddled with huge expectations—expectations I fail to meet, ushering in guilt and shame. I'm pretty good at carrying maidens for five miles.

"Of course, if you treat yourself that way, two things happen. First, the incongruence between the truth of my being and the way of my being makes me sick inside. Second, that sickness leaks out and contaminates others, doing all kinds of violence in the world."

Getting to the truth of your being—to your Essential Self—is critical to knowing yourself.

KNOW THYSELF

You can't lead others until you can lead yourself. You can't love others until you can love yourself. And you can't lead or love yourself until you make some fundamental changes in how you wire your mind, and that starts with knowing who you are being.

This is not a new idea. The words "Know Thyself" were carved over the entry to the temple at Delphi, where Greek kings and queens went to get their tragic questions answered by the Oracle. The trouble was, those leaders would look up at that inscription and they would smile and nod and say, "That's nice."

Then they'd go in and pay a lot of money for advice from the Oracle. In most cases, the answer they got back was a riddle. It never made any sense. The irony is, had they truly known themselves, they could have answered their own questions. Or, even more important, they would have asked the right ones.

The priestesses who ran the Oracle were no dummies. They had things very well thought out. They put the temple way up on top of a mountain, so you had a lot of time to think as you climbed up. The idea of a long hike up a mountain was to help you still your mind. With your head bowed as you stepped up the trail, you would be engaged in your physical body and with your breath, and your mind would calm down.

And then you reach the top, where the temple is. What are you supposed to see on a mountaintop? You're supposed to have a better view of things, the long view, the view from above the battleground. You go to the mountaintop to have deep insights, not to ask poorly considered questions. You stand on the mountain and take a deep breath. You think about the question you are asking. You think about why you're asking it and what you really want to know: the question behind the question. You ask who you are being. You take a moment to get quiet inside so you can hear yourself think.

After all that, when you reach the door of the temple

and see those words over the entry—Know Thyself—you can stop, because you've probably just answered your own question.

**If I had an hour to solve a problem,
I would spend the first fifty-five
minutes identifying the problem and
the last five minutes solving it.**

—ALBERT EINSTEIN

Lasting change begins with the ability to know yourself. But suppose you don't have time to climb a mountain every time you need clarity? This is the killer question that can give you the view from an everyday vantage point.

WHO ARE YOU BEING?

This question is the core of radical self-awareness.

The language is very specific. It's not about who you want to be, who you ought to be, or who you aspire to be. Those are irrelevant ideas. The only thing you must ask is *Who am I being right now, right here, in this moment?* That's all.

Maybe you're irritated. Maybe you're balanced. Maybe you're completely hunky-dory. Which is it? You need to know. Maybe you're about to blow your top. Maybe you're looking for a way to avoid bad news. Maybe you're freaking out. If you don't know who you are being, you're heading for a fall.

Who you are being is important. But it's not as important as *knowing* who you are being. In the moment that you truly know who you are being, you can change.

When I coach leaders of giant organizations, this is where we start. Every morning when you wake up, ask yourself this question. Ask it every moment of the day, from the moment you get to work until the moment your head hits the pillow. Before you write that email, pick up that phone, or walk into that meeting. Every time you walk through a door.

Who are you being?

Take a CEO we'll call Brad. He was in his late fifties when he was named CEO of a Fortune 500 company that produced many of the iconic brands you find in the dairy case of every grocery store in North America. Those famous products were housed in two divisions that got all the investor attention. He had been a division president of the third division that produced the basic dairy products.

The board decided the company was top heavy, so they spun off the two consumer product divisions, providing huge payoffs for investors. They left Brad and his division management team to run the still-giant company, traded on the New York Stock Exchange, that produced an outsized share of the dairy products in the United States.

I was called in because, other than Brad, no one on the executive team had ever been in the C-suite of a public company. The scrutiny was intense, the problems were daunting, and the tension was overwhelming. I had worked with Brad a few years before, and he trusted that I could help his team get their heads turned in the right direction.

In my first meeting with him after he took the top seat, we talked about the challenges.

"I feel like I'm on stage," he said. "It's the constant scrutiny. Not just in the press, not just with investors. It's with everyone. Every time I walk down the hallway, people are watching me, and I'm wondering if what they see sends the right message."

My response to this statement became the framework for my coaching practice and for this book.

"OK," I told him, "here's what you do: every time you stand up from that desk, I want you to pause. Every time you reach for your phone or start to respond to an email, you have to pause. And you have to take inventory of who you're being. And then you have to see if that's who you want to be."

If you don't know who you're being, there's nothing you can do to change it. Who you're being isn't some hidden, mystical state known only to your deepest self. The rest of us can see it plainly on you. You wear it like a sandwich board.

What Brad and every leader like him experiences is the profound impact their presence has on everyone around them. It isn't just the statements they release from the corner office or the speeches they give at the annual meeting. The real communications we make to each other are generated from deep inside.

Every moment, with every thought and action, you're sending a message to the world around you. That message will either be sent by your Essential Self or it will be sent by your Synthetic Self. And your Synthetic Self always gets it wrong.

Knowing who you are being changes the way the rest of the world experiences you.

ASKING WHO YOU ARE BEING *CHANGES* WHO YOU ARE BEING

You will soon find that just asking the question puts your mind into an alert, focused state, and that's where the Essential Self is found.

People who practice radical self-awareness operate from a state of present clarity. They are more perceptive and able to read beyond people's words to understand what people are truly asking. When you can understand the people around you—when you identify who *they* are being and what *they* want—you can help them fulfill their own destinies, which is what leadership really is.

JOY IS NOTHING MORE THAN THE PERFECT PRESENCE OF SELF. IT'S NOT AS HARD AS WE THINK.

Asking who you are being is a call to attention. Paying attention to your attention changes the quality of your perception. You are able to experience the moment from a different point of view, as if you had just stepped outside of yourself and are watching yourself from the other side of the room. You have stepped out of your Synthetic Self, which fights to mask who you are being and to protect the ego. Just making that shift—that act of "changing minds," as Frank Allen put it—changes who you are being. It answers the question without the need for words.

Changing who you are being changes how other people perceive and interact with you. They may not be aware of why their experience of you changes or how their behavior shifts. And it's not important that they be. Whether they know it or not, they can feel the difference between a sense of presence and someone who projects a false impression.

We can feel when someone is acting from their Essential Self.

Who you are being—if you're being radically self-aware, if you're being intensely curious about the person in front of you, if you're reading them with whole-hearted acceptance and appreciation—can change not only how they see you but who they become in your presence.

SITTING IN JUDGMENT

For a number of years, I've coached young litigators on how to make an opening argument that sticks—but it may be a waste of time. In theory, a trial begins at the end of jury selection, though many senior litigators will tell you that by that point, the trial is already over.

As the members of the jury pool wait for the selection process to begin, they have nothing to do but observe the people at the front of the courtroom. The jurors create their own impressions of the case based on the body language of the lawyers, judge, and defendants, and on their own biases. Each member of the pool has a subjective understanding of the case before it even begins, often without realizing it.

At the Max Planck Institute in Berlin, John-Dylan Haynes has been doing studies on the science of decision-making. In a 2008 study, Dr. Haynes set up a test in which participants were asked to push a button. They could push the button with either hand, but they were asked to remember the moment they made the left or right decision. As the researchers recorded their brain activity on an MRI scan, they discovered something interesting. The decision of which hand to use was made as much as seven to ten seconds before the subject was aware of his or her choice.

"Many processes in the brain occur automatically and without involvement of our consciousness," Dr. Haynes said in an interview in *Nature Neuroscience*. "This prevents our mind from being overloaded by simple routine tasks. But when it comes to decisions, we tend to assume they are made by our conscious mind. This is questioned by our current findings."

In other words, we make decisions in our unconscious mind and then rationalize those decisions in our rational mind. That's not to say that we can't override those unconscious decisions. We can. It starts with pausing to ask the third question: *Who am I being?*

HOW LONG DOES IT TAKE TO CHANGE YOUR MIND?

If you've seen Harold Ramis's classic comedy, *Groundhog Day*, you know the power of being able to fully know and change who you are being. In the film, Bill Murray plays Phil Connors, a miserable and arrogant man who is almost universally disliked. A weatherman for a local TV station, he's sent to Punxsutawney, Pennsylvania, to cover Groundhog Day. Phil tries to leave town but is stranded by an unexpected blizzard. When he wakes up the next morning, it's Groundhog Day all over again. Literally. We soon discover that it's going to be Groundhog Day every day until Phil finally learns how to love. And, to put it in the language of this book, he can't do that until he learns who he's being.

The genius of the movie lies in this question: What if time stood still for as long as it took for you to really know and appreciate the miracle of who you are as a human being, and then, when you got it, it would all start up again and you could go on with your one wild and precious life, living every day fully present to everyone around you?

Phil's journey from self-loathing to self-knowledge, from being miserable to Being Essential, is the same journey each of us takes throughout our lives. It doesn't matter how long it takes. All that matters is that we get there. We get there when we learn who we are being in each moment.

> Mastery of your thoughts is essential
> for your enlightenment.
>
> —PAUL FERRINI

KEEP CROSSING THE RIVER

The story of the two monks is a parable about the duality of your own mind. The monk who carried the woman five miles and the monk who put her down are two sides of the same mind, the side that lives in fear and attachment and the side that is free of both. The young monk is the Synthetic Self, always judging and unsure. The older monk is the Essential Self, always present and aware.

Thousands of times each day, your mind flips from the Synthetic to the Essential Self. You scream at someone in traffic (the judgmental monk) and instantly notice what you're doing (the *essential* monk). The gravity of the ego is powerful. We've cultivated it for so many years that it holds us hostage. The Essential Self, on the other hand, doesn't care what the ego does, because it understands that the ego isn't real. It's just something your mind makes up.

So, remember this: we have a choice in who we are being and we can change it, with practice, in an instant, with a single question. Just asking who you are being changes who you are being. It is the foundation of awareness.

You can be a master of many things,
but to be a master of your Self is
the most important of them all.

—BIJOY GOSWAMI

WHAT
do you
WANT?

Don't ask the world to change . . . you change first.

—ANTHONY DE MELLO

THE TURNING POINT

YOU'VE NOW REACHED THE HEART of the Being Essential practice, the pivot where you can change not only yourself but your relationship to the world around you.

The first three questions are about connecting with your precious Essential Self.

First, you located yourself. You identified where you are.

Then, you identified why you are there. You identified the choices that brought you to the place you find yourself. And you also identified what the moment is asking of you.

You used your radical self-awareness to see who you are being and, once you know who you are being and which mind you're operating from, discovered that you can change.

The last three questions in the practice are about testing your thinking and your choices.

At this pivot point, in question four, we ask, *What do you want?* Not over the span of your life, not for lunch, not in your wardrobe, but in *this* moment.

You want to rip somebody's head off? Maybe. But is that *really* what you want? Probably not. Probably what you really want is a problem solved. A relationship improved. Or a moment of transformation. What you probably want is to feel better about yourself. This question, like the previous one, is focused on the present.

Together, questions three and four provide the fulcrum for changing our minds. Asking who you are being changes who you are being. And in that state of presence, asking what you want changes what you want.

With practice, you'll find that this question—with the one before it—becomes a switch that you can use to right yourself. Brad, the CEO we met in the last chapter, worried that his stress level was interfering with his ability to lead effectively. Asking who he was being helped him reset his self-awareness so he could recognize when he was acting from stress. When he added question four, he had a deep realization. It wasn't that he wanted to protect his staff from his stress. What he wanted was to stop feeling fearful and not quite good enough to be CEO. He wanted to shed his Synthetic Self and step into his expanded leadership role. Although he didn't know how to express it at first, he wanted to experience the perfect presence of self.

Remember the story of my Essential Child, perched on the jungle gym, intent on not missing a moment of the sunset? What I thought I wanted was to possess the sunset. But, more essentially, I wanted to be whole and complete in myself. At eight years old, I didn't know what that meant. But today, when I ask myself who I am being and what I want, there is a single answer. There may be lots of words I can use to describe it, but it all comes down to this: I want to be my Essential Self.

With practice, these two questions—*Who are you being?* and *What do you want?*—become as one. And this is where the Essential Self is found.

HOW DO YOU ASK FOR WHAT YOU WANT?

Don't misunderstand this point: just asking the question probably won't get you what you want. Identifying that you want to go to medical school doesn't make you a doctor. And even deciding in your mind that that's what you want doesn't mean you've found the genuine answer.

A good interviewer will tell you it takes three tries to get a real answer from someone you're questioning. The first time you ask someone, for instance, "What do you want?" you get a superficial answer: "I want to go for a walk up to the top of the hill." The second time you ask, maybe changing the wording a little, you get a more thoughtful response as the person digs a little deeper. The third time, with luck, you get something that comes from an authentic place: "I've been under a lot of stress lately. I just want to get somewhere where I can look out at the view and find myself."

With practice, leaders, coaches, and reporters can become great interviewers. But no interview is harder than the interviews we have with ourselves.

A CHARACTER IN SEARCH OF A STORY

A writer friend asked me to read a screenplay she had written. She wanted my opinion on what I thought it needed.

The manuscript she handed me was an autobiographical story based on a journey the writer made in 1977 when she was a young mother in Dallas, down on her luck. In the screenplay, the woman needs a break and needs some money. When a friend tells her there's a company that builds ambulances and needs someone to deliver one to Boston, she jumps at the chance.

What followed was one of the most amazing series of events I've ever read. A breakdown an hour out of town. A tornado not long after that. Dents, dings, and scratches on the new paint. Driving through Memphis before dawn as the radio announces that Elvis has died. In Nashville, a multiple car pileup. More dents. Side trips. Help from truckers she meets on the CB radio. A drunk driver crashes into the truck in front of her. Trucks on fire, one loaded with charcoal briquets. The story had everything but the marshmallows! And still the woman has to get the nearly totaled ambulance to Boston.

Like I said, an amazing series of events and the setup for a comic road movie to rival everything from *It Happened One Night* to *Planes, Trains, and Automobiles*. It had all that, but it wasn't a *story* yet.

In a story, the woman behind the wheel has to want something. And always, what she thinks she wants on page one turns out not to be what she wants at all. The story is how she discovers what it is that she really wants, which is transformation.

In the road trip we just described, the heroine might start out wanting nothing more than a break from the tedium of her life and some cash in her pocket. Halfway through, she'll have more at stake: she'll be focused on staying alive.

At the end, she'll realize her deepest desire, which is to turn her life around, quit being the victim of her bad choices, and work toward the kind of life she now knows she deserves and can create.

I handed the screenplay back and shared my thoughts with my friend. But even as we talked, I knew we weren't really talking about the screenplay, which would be easy to fix. We were talking about her continuing journey in life, the transformation she was hoping to find through her writing, the perilous hero's journey she is on to keep from crashing and burning as she finds out who she is being and what she wants.

Now *that's* a story.

All good things . . . come by grace and grace comes by art and art does not come easy.

—NORMAN MACLEAN

Look at the stories we've shared in the previous chapters.

In Elmore Leonard's *The Switch*, Mickey thinks she wants the men (and boy) in her life to stop acting like obnoxious jerks. But underneath that, there's the beginning of a personal seismic shift: she's starting to suspect that she's been playing nice all her life and that underneath this construction of a self, there's a real self, trying to kick its way out.

By the middle of the book, that's exactly what she does—she kicks one of the kidnappers in the groin and makes her escape. And by the end of the novel, the escape is complete and Mickey is on the way to becoming the person she wants to be, not the person she let everyone else set her up to be.

In *Scent of a Woman*, Frank Slade starts off thinking he knows what he wants: he wants to finish the bottle of Scotch he's drinking, then head to Manhattan for a last lost weekend before he takes his life. He's hired a prep school kid to shepherd him through his last laugh, and halfway through the movie, Frank becomes interested in helping the kid grow a little backbone. By the end of the movie, he knows his deepest desire is to be the kind of man others will respect, the man he can finally become because of what he's learned about himself. The irony is that his blindness helps him see that.

In *The Apartment*, C.C. Baxter just wants to get back into his apartment so he can get some sleep. As the story progresses, he gets ambitious and thinks he wants to rise through the ranks of the corporation so he can get the girl. At the middle of the story, when he and the doctor in the next apartment are reviving Miss Kubelik after she ingests his sleeping pills, the doctor says to him, "Why don't you be a mensch, Baxter? You know what that is? A real human being." By the end of the movie, when Baxter realizes that's exactly who he wants to be, he doesn't have to go after the girl. The girl comes to him.

And in *Groundhog Day*, Phil Connors wants to move to a major-market TV station where he'll make more money and be more famous, thinking that will earn him the respect he wants from other people. In the middle of the movie, stuck in his time warp and living the same day over and over again, he thinks he can seduce a woman by dating her over and over until he finds the secret to charming her. But in the end, he learns so much about her, and everyone else in the town, that he realizes the only thing worth having is love. And when he learns how to truly love another human being, he's released to get on with his life with the woman he loves.

Throughout all of literature and all of movies, the through-line of every story is the journey of the characters moving from what they think they want to what they really want. If a character knows what she wants from the beginning and goes after it, that's not much of a character—it's not much of a story. What makes a story human is a journey of self-discovery and the subsequent work to achieve one's dreams.

In every story, what the hero really wants is to find the most essential version of the self.

Every person has a story. Every person you love, every person you lead is chasing things they think they want. Sometimes we get clarity on what we really want, which is great. But most of the time, clarity is hard to find.

The famed Hollywood screenwriter and story consultant Blake Snyder once said, "If life gives you horseshit, look for the pony." Here's what you need to know for your story to get on track to a satisfying ending: in virtually every case, *you're* the pony.

We are so accustomed to disguise
ourselves to others that, in the end,
we become disguised to ourselves.

—FRANÇOIS VI, DUC DE LA ROCHEFOUCAULD

WHAT YOU WANT IN THE MOMENT DEFINES THE MOMENT

What you want in the moment defines not only that moment but every moment that follows. You cannot separate what you want from who you are being. Anything you *say* you want is irrelevant (and unsatisfying) unless it arises from who you're authentically being.

Let's say you're angry with a family member. You're incensed by something they said. You identify who you're being: you're angry and offended. Fine. Now: *What do you want?*

If you say, "I want her to apologize," that's irrelevant because you've skipped right over the only person that matters in the interaction. This isn't about the family member. This is about you (you're the pony!). Someone said something and you constructed a reaction to what she said. That reaction was painful to you and you made yourself a victim of your own reaction. You did that to yourself. Is that what you want? Of course not. But we spend most of our lives *thinking* that's what we want.

If you say, "I don't want to feel this way," that is authentic. That is you understanding that you have agency in your feelings. But does it make you feel better? It's a start. And if you say, "I want to feel joyful instead of angry," suddenly you can have access to your Essential Self. You can put your Essential Self in the driver's seat and let her steer.

From this vantage point, through the lens of *essentiality*, you remap your own hero's journey toward what matters most in each moment. This simple internal shift may seem almost insignificant, but the returns can be meaningful. You can still pursue the more tangible things you want: that doctorate, or to make sure everyone's on track for the Q2 launch of the product update, or to finish that screenplay you've been struggling with. The difference is that you'll be pursuing your goals and delivering your results with conscious self-leadership.

Discover what you really want on your journey and keep coming back to it. Make that the story of your life.

**To truly live is so startling it leaves
little time for anything else.**

—EMILY DICKINSON

WHAT
wants to
HAPPEN?

Innovation occurs when ripe seeds
fall on fertile ground.

—WALTER ISAACSON

LIVING IN TOUCH WITH OUR TIMES

UNDERSTANDING WHAT WANTS TO HAPPEN in the world around you is a critical self-awareness skill. It is at the intersection of internal and external awareness that you can make a profound difference in your life and in the world.

In 1937, something wanted to happen. In universities and labs around the world, scientists and mathematicians were working on the same idea: the design of a machine that could be used to perform logical, computational tasks. The idea wasn't a new one: a hundred years earlier, Charles Babbage had published a paper about the Analytical Engine he was designing to solve mathematical problems, and Ada Lovelace was working with him on programming the device to solve problems of logic. In the 1880s, Herman Hollerith built a punch card machine that reduced the time needed to tabulate US census results from eight years by hand to just one year by machine. By 1937, both the need for computing power and the technologies to make it a reality had merged to create a tipping point.

Fear of a pending war had scientists thinking about things like weather patterns, artillery trajectory tables, the math for advanced physics, and other fast-moving scientific advances. For all of these efforts, they needed a way to speed mathematical computations.

In *The Innovators*, his book about the birth of the digital age, Walter Isaacson writes:

> Instead of having a single cause, the great advances
> of 1937 came from a combination of capabilities,

ideas, and needs that coincided in multiple places. As often happens in the annals of invention, especially information technology invention, the time was right and the atmosphere was charged. The development of vacuum tubes for the radio industry paved the way for the creation of electronic digital circuits. That was accompanied by theoretical advances in logic that made circuits more useful. And the march was quickened by the drums of war. As nations began arming for the looming conflict, it became clear that computational power was as important as firepower. Advances fed on one another, occurring almost simultaneously and spontaneously, at Harvard and MIT, at Princeton and Bell Labs, in an apartment in Berlin, and even in a basement in Ames, Iowa.

In other words, big, powerful computers wanted to happen. And those who understood that—those who were asking where they were on the arc of development and looking for clues that could lead them to the next development—they were the ones who moved the science forward and applied it to solving (and sometimes unintentionally creating) real-world problems. In the context of the Being Essential practice, they had a profound sense of each of the questions: they knew where they were (at a tipping point in technological development), they knew why they were there (to give birth to a new scientific age), they knew who they were being (deeply focused on the possibilities of the moment), and they were very clear on what they wanted (they wanted to be on the leading edge of this change). And question five? In the conversations they were having with each other and the experimental work they were doing— even in the hours spent doing advanced mathematics by hand—it must have been like watching a door open to the future. Only it was no longer the future. They had brought progress into the present.

Synchronicity is being intensely open to what wants to happen next.

Fast-forward twenty years, to October 4, 1957, when the Soviet Union launched into orbit a satellite they called *Sputnik*. It was the height of the Cold War, when fear of war with Russia was so present that we taught schoolchildren to "duck and cover" beneath their desks, for all the good that would have done against a nuclear attack.

In response, President Dwight D. Eisenhower appointed MIT president James Killian to be the White House science advisor. Working with the secretary of defense, Killian arranged for the Defense Advanced Research Projects Agency (DARPA) to be placed under the command of the Pentagon to study how computers around the country could be connected to each other to speed the flow of information, innovation, and research.

Once again, in labs and universities around the world—but primarily in the United States and Britain—there were scientists, engineers, and big thinkers working on the idea of a network of computers. Universities were involved because many researchers were fascinated with the idea of connected personal computers that could augment human intelligence. Corporations were involved because the military contracted them to research the concept and because they saw a market opportunity. And the military was involved for a variety of reasons, from speeding research related to the space race to providing a resilient information network that could survive a nuclear attack.

That was the birth of a movement that led to the creation and expansion of the internet. For those who shared in the idea, who saw that a world of interconnected personal computers wanted to happen, the dawn of the information age would forever change their careers, their fortunes, and the world.

Sensing what wants to happen is not limited to physicists. Asian cultures evolved with a somewhat different way of looking at the nature of the times in which we live. Marie-Louise von Franz, a Swiss psychologist, wrote about the way Chinese cultures sense what wants to happen. "As soon as we notice that certain types of events 'like' to cluster together at certain times," she wrote, "we begin to understand the attitude of the Chinese, whose theories of medicine, philosophy, and even building are based on a 'science' of meaningful coincidences. The classical Chinese texts did not ask what causes what, but rather what 'likes' to occur with what."

Joshua Cooper Ramo offered a similar assessment of the cultural differences in his book *The Seventh Sense: Power, Fortune, and Survival in the Age of Networks*. Ramo worked and studied in China for a number of years and developed a unique feel for the difference between Western and Chinese culture.

"When Chinese want to do something, we begin with the question 'What is the nature of the age?'" he writes. "Westerners begin with the goal. What do they aim to achieve? Chinese tend to look at any problem they face and begin by considering the conditions and environment around the problem. The context matters as much as the solution because, even if you think you've solved a specific problem, that context endures."

Here is why these examples of pre-sensing matter: in all of the scenarios, people sensed something that was going to emerge. They *pre-sensed* it. Then they brought it into the present. Your practice will lead you to do the same in your life.

PRE-SENSING THE FUTURE

Otto Scharmer teaches at MIT's Sloan School of Management and is the founder of The Presencing Institute, which brings together leaders from around the world who are interested in developing what he describes as "an intimate relationship with the emerging future."

"To me," he writes in *Presence: Human Purpose and the Field of the Future* (coauthored with Peter Senge, Betty Sue Flowers, and Joseph Jaworski), "presencing is about 'pre-sensing' and bringing into presence—and into the present—your highest future potential. It's not just 'the future' in some abstract sense but my own highest future possibility as a human being."

Think of question five as drawing a direct and very bold line from the world your Essential Child looked out upon to the world that you are about to step into. That future reality—your own "highest future possibility"—is what this question wants you to discover.

To do this requires a dual focus: internal and external. The internal focus is on things you are thinking about, consciously and subconsciously, usually regarding your work, your significant relationships, or the coaching work you're doing to identify and live in your Essential Self. The external focus is a kind of radar seeking to link your internal quest with the world around you. Your mind should be on the lookout for external connections to help you solve the internal quest. Think of this as the Essential Self on a journey of discovery, driven by a vision of a future state— a constant, ears-up search for signposts in the world of ideas, personas, and activities that are external to your mind. Your mind is not searching for confirmation of internal biases; it is searching for synergy. Intuitively, we want to complete a loop within our psyche by connecting to events that occur outside the self. Completing the loop helps us feel that we are not separate from the world around us; we are of the world.

Eastern philosophers have also explored how we become more self-aware by seeking the crossroads of our internal and external minds. The most ancient Buddhist texts call this intersection *tathagata-garbha*, the matrix of the temporal and the transcendent. In this matrix, we can develop the capacity for presencing ideas, experiences, and interactions that are waiting to happen. At the *tathagata-garbha* is the opportunity to give birth to the future. It opens the doors to *co-incidence*, bringing two separate incidents, one temporal and one transcendent, into being in the present moment. It opens the door to *synchronicity*, which is the experience of noticing and experiencing what wants to happen next.

We do not create our destiny; we participate in its unfolding. Synchronicity works as a catalyst toward the working out of that destiny.

—DAVID RICHO

LIVING A LIFE OF SYNCHRONICITY

The word *synchronicity*, as we use it here, was coined by Carl Jung in his 1952 book, *Synchronicity: An Acausal Connecting Principle*. Jung's ideas were sparked during dinners with Albert Einstein when they were both young men and later by his decades-long conversations with the Nobel-laureate physicist Wolfgang Pauli. All three of these remarkable scientists were interested in the parallels between their respective fields, between the physical and psychic (meaning *of the psyche*, not ESP or mind-reading) dimensions of reality. Just as the human mind contains powerful stores of energy and knowledge that are invisible to us, so does the structure of the atom and all the parts of mass and energy that make it up. Like the Buddhists, the scientists noticed the connections between the temporal and transcendent realities that make up our world.

"The radioactive nucleus is an excellent symbol for the source of energy of the collective unconscious," Jung wrote in a letter to Pauli in 1935, "the ultimate external stratum of which appears as individual consciousness. As a symbol, it indicates that consciousness does not grow out of any activity that is inherent to it; rather, it is constantly being produced by an energy that comes from the depths of the unconscious and has thus been depicted in the form of rays since time immemorial."

Jung is suggesting that, at some level we don't fully understand, we live in a matrix of consciousness where experiences can be more than just coincidence, where our internal experience intersects with external occurrences. According to Jung and Pauli, it is as if your psyche is looking for something and, at the same time, that something is looking for you. Your curiosity is the key to those *somethings* finding each other. Not to ascribe volition to external events (although many do, including Jung and scholars of virtually all religions), but our psyche can attach meaning to, and derive value from, seemingly coincidental events that seem to want to happen, just when we need them to.

The more deeply you are able to locate yourself through the radical self-awareness of these questions and the deeper you can go into who you are being and what you want, the more frequently you will experience these coincidences that open the doors you need, just when you need them.

Our advisory company, Reservoir LLC, was created by an ongoing series of these sorts of coincidences. I was interested in expanding my individual practice as an executive coach into a circle of coaches and advisors that could offer more resources than I could on my own. In a chance encounter at a conference, I took an empty seat at a table and fell into a conversation with another consultant who liked my idea of an advisory circle. A few months later, she was at a conference when a third consultant, the former CEO of a global publishing house, took another empty seat. He had become a CEO coach in his retirement, and when she shared our idea, he wanted in. At another conference, I was seated next to a leadership expert from Harvard who then became part of our circle. A contract to help a graduate management professor from The New School speak about a new book led to a relationship with another member of the circle. A call to a young MBA friend to help manage a small project led to a new generation of thought leadership, and she became our head of strategy and innovation. On and on, in coincidental meeting after coincidental meeting, a new and vibrant company emerged. It emerged at the intersection of what all of us were looking for, and what our clients, leaders of businesses, universities, and nonprofits were looking for.

This kind of emergence of a group comes from what Scharmer and his colleagues call "the broadcasting of intention," where a number of people are sensing a need and a possibility and are thus drawn toward others with the same sense. We had similar ideas, similar intentions, and were looking, whether we quite knew it or not, for a connection with others who shared that intention.

Knowing where you are is where this work starts. And knowing how to think about why you're here, who you're being, and what you want opens the gateway to this sense of what wants to happen next.

Here's an example of how that works. On the day I was rewriting this section of the book, looking to provide deeper clarity, I stopped to prepare for an interview with Danica Reinicke, a climate scientist working with Smartfin, a nonprofit group studying the decline of coral beds around the world and using tourism—and in particular, traveling surfers—to help gather data on temperatures and water conditions. While I was looking at her website, I noticed a post for a video called *Chasing Coral*. Below the title, a subtitle: *What lies below reveals what lies ahead.* In the context of the video, it referred to the use of data to predict climate change. But in the context of this work and the question *What wants to happen?* it was a beautiful metaphor for the process of unlocking the future.

What lies below—our connection with our Essential Self—*reveals what lies ahead*—what wants to happen based on the intention our Essential Self is broadcasting.

So what wants to happen in your life? What intention are you broadcasting? When you look at what lies below, the depth of your radical self-awareness will soon reveal what lies ahead.

PRACTICING BEING ESSENTIAL

It begins with quieting the mind. The quiet mind is found in slowing down the breath and observing your thoughts, learning to ignore any that emerge from your Synthetic Self. As you exhale, imagine you're sending your breath out through the roof of your mouth and blowing up a balloon in your cranium. As the balloon expands, it pushes all non-essential thoughts out to the edges of your mind, where it becomes easy to see that they are unhelpful.

Now, begin moving through the questions.

Where am I? In the quiet center of my mind.

Why am I here? To connect with my Essential Self.

Who am I being? I am being curious about what's under all these random thoughts.

What do I want? I want to find what lies below and what lies ahead.

Is it as simple as that? Yes and no. Simplicity takes practice and patience. It calls us to dig deeper with every breath.

When we went through the Being Essential framework with a client, something interesting happened when we arrived at question five. A young man in his mid-thirties, our client had come up out of a tough early childhood determined to make something of himself. He had an impressive career going but was filled with the feeling that he hadn't made it far enough, that he was running out of time.

He felt he was in the coaching program to make some decisions on self-improvement. When I asked what he wanted, he said, "I want clarity on how to accomplish my goals."

But when we reached this question, *What wants to happen?* he seemed confused for a moment.

"Nothing," he said.

"Nothing?"

"OK," he said, "obstruction and status quo. Nothing seems to change."

I asked him to step back and take a look from a different angle, the angle of a small boy walking along the shoreline of a lake. He had told me this story when he was doing his Essential Child exercise. Standing on the shoreline near where he was camping with his family, he looked up to see beautiful houses on a bluff above him, and he knew that someday he would live up there. Sure enough, by the time he was thirty, he was financially secure enough to return to the lake and buy the very house he had gazed upon as a boy. He married a woman who came from a well-to-do background and who loved and respected him. He was a rising star in his industry. That poor boy by the lake had climbed a long, long way.

"From this angle," I said, "it looks like nothing but continued success wants to happen for you. Why are you focused on obstacles?"

In that exchange, he was able to uncover something profound about the way he saw himself: in spite of all his success, he still lived inside a Synthetic Self of his own creation, a self-concept where he was cast as a failure, as if all his successes had to be measured (and devalued) by a standard just past what he had achieved.

What wants to happen in his life is growth and success. What would it take for him to see that the doors to his future are open wide? All he has to do is keep moving forward.

NOT EVERYTHING WE WANT WANTS TO HAPPEN

For a person who's nine months pregnant, childbirth almost always wants to happen. For someone who goes skydiving, coming down to the ground always wants to happen. Fall asleep at the wheel on a country road, and you'll likely end up in a cornfield (if you're lucky). There are many chains of action that are predictable.

But there are many more endeavors where the outcomes are not guaranteed. Writing a book you hope will be a best seller. Starting a business you hope will be embraced by customers. Presenting a new sales compensation plan to your team. Asking someone out on a date. None of these are slam-dunk certainties that end with you getting what you want.

Almost everyone has experienced meeting someone they like, sensing the other person likes them too, and feeling they have a lot in common. It feels like the beginning of a great relationship. And then, nothing happens. Maybe one of you ghosts. Maybe timing is not on your side. And so nothing ever comes of the relationship. Just because we want something to happen doesn't mean it's going to. Most of us learned this in kindergarten, or from the Rolling Stones.

The fifth question provides a reality check. Having a strong sense of what wants to happen—and what doesn't—can validate what you believe you want and help you design a plan to overcome obstacles if you feel strongly that you're on the right path.

We are put on earth for a little space that
we might learn to bear the beams of love.

—WILLIAM BLAKE

Asking what wants to happen next is a call to work on sensing what wants to happen around you and where you fit in. This means developing your intuitive mindset, so that you begin asking better questions about what you're doing and what results you want.

The classic Japanese novel *Musashi* by Eiji Yoshikawa has spawned dozens of movies, TV series, and manga. It follows the early journey of the legendary swordsman Miyamoto Musashi as he learns the true Way of the Samurai. At one point, early in the book, after he's downed a seemingly invincible opponent with a single blow, a wise monk takes Musashi aside and tells him that his strength is his problem, that he needs to control his strength and become weaker. Of course, this advice baffles the young warrior. Isn't the point of all his training to be the strongest one?

But soon he learns otherwise. Sometimes we should storm the castle; sometimes we should sit quietly and wait for the castle to open its doors to us. When we don't have a clear sense of what wants to happen, we may try to bend the future to our own will. When we sense that we are part of the larger world and its intricate connections, we understand that the best course of action may be to prepare ourselves for open doors.

And isn't that why you are here?

**Tomorrow belongs to those
who can hear it coming.**

—DAVID BOWIE

WHAT
don't you
KNOW?

Unlearn what you think you know so that
you can relearn what you need to know.

—MARGIE WARRELL

THE FINE ART OF NOT KNOWING

THINK OF A TIME WHEN you had a deep misunderstanding of a situation. You heard someone say something or saw someone do something, and you interpreted it in a way that was not aligned with reality. You thought you knew what was happening and later learned you were completely wrong. Maybe it was a moment that didn't mean much. Or maybe it was a moment that meant everything, a missed chance to change your world.

But what if you were to discover that much, even most, of what you know—all the knowledge you have gathered throughout your entire life—is not true? Earlier in this book, in "The Practice of Radical Self-Awareness," we learned about the Synthetic Self, the persona we all create to protect our ego. Everything that Synthetic Self has convinced you that you know is probably false.

All of our lives, we make the mistake of thinking that we know what is true, and so often we are wrong. Yet, we spend so much time affirming our assumptions and confirming our biases that we actually create our own reality. Radical self-awareness demands that we constantly check at the door what we believe we know and become deeply curious about what we don't know.

The first five questions are about identifying what you need to know: knowing where you are and why you're here, who you're being and what you want, what wants to happen on your journey and in the world around you. Now we have a question that's all about not knowing.

Let's return to Martin Buber's story about the rabbi and the police chief who had a question:

If God knows everything, why did he ask Adam "Where are you?"

"Adam hides to avoid having to account for himself," Buber explains, "and to evade taking responsibility for his life. Likewise, every person hides, because every person is Adam, in Adam's quandary. Every person rebuilds his existence as a network of hiding places in order to escape taking responsibility for life lived. . . . This creates a new situation, which from day to day and from one hiding place to the next becomes more and more untenable."

Buber is saying that we hide because we don't want to know who and where we are, believing that if we don't know, we don't have to take responsibility. When we create comfortable hiding places in order to dodge the more difficult work of self-awareness, we end up with a facsimile of the Essential Self—a Synthetic Self—and usually this invented self is vastly misaligned with who we truly are. Still, the Synthetic Self believes it knows us and knows what is true about our world—it must if it is to maintain its illusion.

But here's the paradox: the danger of not knowing is nothing compared to the trap of knowing. When you think about it, what is the biggest impediment to knowledge? It's knowing. Albert Einstein spoke constantly of the need to assume you don't know, even with something as seemingly provable as mathematics. "As far as the laws of mathematics refer to reality," he said, "they are not certain; and as far as they are certain, they do not refer to reality." Einstein stressed the need to start with questions and not answers. His genius was his ability to keep his mind open to undiscovered possibilities.

A person who has all the answers ends up with none of the questions. A person who thinks she knows what's going on is likely to either miss or misinterpret everything that's happening around her. We think we know, and so we each create our own special misinterpretation of life. It's no wonder we find it difficult to understand one another sometimes!

> In the beginner's mind there
> are many possibilities, but in
> the expert's there are few.
> —SHUNRYU SUZUKI

Shunryu Suzuki, a Japanese teacher who in 1959 established the Zen Center in San Francisco, once said, "If your mind is empty, it is always ready for anything; it is open to everything. In the beginner's mind there are many possibilities; in the expert's mind there are few."

We're not talking about a mind that is unread or uneducated or a mind that cannot function in a thoughtful way.

Being able to ask *What don't I know?* means that you are disciplined to distinguish thoughts that are generated and perpetuated by the Synthetic Self from those of the Essential Self.

THE MAN WHO KNEW NOTHING

In sixth-century China, during the Liang Dynasty, the Emperor Wu enthusiastically promoted Buddhism throughout the land. He became a monk and built beautiful temples. One day, he heard there was a traveling monk in the area, a Buddhist teacher who had walked all the way from India to share ideas about the nature of the Buddha mind. So, with great interest, the emperor sent for him.

He showed the monk all the good works he'd done: the sacred texts he'd read, his shaved head, his orange robes. He asked the monk, "Look at all I've done. What's the karmic value of this?"

And the monk said, "None whatsoever."

This answer surprised the emperor, who asked, "Then how do you get karmic value?"

The monk said, "I don't know."

Now the emperor was confused. He'd been told that this particular monk was quite senior and a real scholar. It made no sense that such a teacher would not know the answer to such a basic tenet of the teachings.

So he asked, "Then who stands before me?"

And the monk said, "I have no idea."

If the answer sounds very Zen to you, that's because the monk was Bodhidharma, the founder of Chan Buddhism, which later evolved into Zen when it reached Japan. He was no doubt a scholar, having been born, according to contemporary accounts, the third son of a great Indian king. The Buddhist tradition was nearly one thousand years old by the time he met the emperor, and Bodhidharma was not only well educated but—of great interest to kung fu movie fans—a founder of the Shaolin Monastery.

So, why did Bodhidharma tell the emperor that he knew nothing? He did this to educate the emperor about the danger of thinking that one knows. The emperor, in his enthusiasm to be the best Buddhist in history, was deeply proud of everything he had done. He was even more proud of all he knew. His knowledge blinded him to that fact that wisdom lies in the ability to admit that we do not know.

The whole problem with the world
is that fools and fanatics are always
so certain of themselves and
wiser people so full of doubts.

—BERTRAND RUSSELL

THE TYRANNY OF KNOWING

In our divided political era, anyone who is not confused doesn't really understand what's going on. Here's why: those on the far edges of the issues of our times, those with the most fixed positions on the critical problems to be solved, know for absolute certain that they are right. They *know*. But because they are locked into their positions, they are unable to understand the perspectives and nuances of today's very complex issues. Because people with fixed political positions are so certain of their ideas, they are unable to understand what is truly going on.

That's a good description of the partisan political divides that afflict many countries today. Well-intentioned people on both sides of partisan spectrums are sure they know what's true. In this state of knowing, they can't understand the position of the other side except to say, "They are crazy and want to destroy our country."

This insistence on knowing lies at the heart of propaganda: a medium that asks illusory questions in order to cement a fixed point of view that cannot be affected by facts. When a propagandist asks a question (and propagandists don't exist only in politics—they are frequently found at family dinners!), he is creating an illusory alternate reality.

When someone in any country asks, "Which party will make us great again?" they are presenting a twist of logic. First, the question assumes we are not great. We may or may not be, but in most countries in the world, there are at least some reasons to celebrate the progress of recent centuries and, indeed, of the last few decades. Second, the question asserts that a political party can "make us great" and limits the choice to only one party. Of course, the party that asks the question limits the choice to itself.

We do this all the time in all our relationships and, most damaging, in our relationship with our selves. Our Synthetic Self might ask, "What can I do to be worthy of love?" The question assumes that we are not worthy of love at all. It asserts that we have to perform an action or be a certain way to be worthy of love and suggests that we are, in fact, probably unable to actually make it happen. The Synthetic Self begins at the point of knowing when in fact it knows nothing.

WHAT WE NEED TO KNOW

There are times when it makes sense to make a list of things we don't know. Firefighters are people who must be adept at not knowing. They are trained to access a long inventory of questions that they cannot answer until they arrive at a scene but need to find out fast: Is anyone in the house? Are there pets inside? Is the house structurally sound enough for a rescue attempt? Are there flammables inside that could explode? How long do we have before the fire spreads to the adjoining houses? Firefighters are trained not to make assumptions because those assumptions could get them killed. They are trained not to know.

Like firefighters, we need to be deeply curious about what we don't know. What you or I don't know may not get us killed, but we would certainly lead richer, more authentic lives if we practiced the art of not knowing. Through asking what we don't know, we move ourselves closer to discovering what is true.

AVOID TRUTHINESS

Daniel Kahneman, the Nobel Prize–winning psychologist, has spent a lifetime studying the ways our minds work. He asks people to think about what it means to know.

"In everyday language," he said in a talk to the National Academy of Science in 2012, "there are two conditions for using the word 'know': the absence of doubt and the truth of the belief." Unfortunately, as he goes on to explain, neither of those conditions contains facts or even truth. "True believers believe that what they believe is true. They 'know' it. From their point of view, science is just a religion and, like all other religions, it's false compared to theirs."

In the same way, scientists think they know what it means to know because they deal with factual data. But even scientists know their minds can act to bias and rewire their thoughts, so that they come, like all of us, to accept things because they *feel* true.

Comedian Stephen Colbert calls this feeling *truthiness*. Truthiness is a way of knowing based on associative thinking. If someone I like, trust, or respect says something, I'm more likely to feel the statement to be true. It may or may not be true in reality, but it has truthiness for me.

As Kahneman explains it, we have a storytelling system hardwired in our minds, and the coherence of stories, rather than facts, leads us to judge what is true.

"Anything that is repeated many times," he says, "is more likely to appear true. Anything that is processed easily is more likely to appear true. If it rhymes, it feels more likely to be true."

Kahneman and Colbert may have very different professions, but their ideas are related: to sort fact from fiction in our own lives and to avoid the trap of knowing, we have to be aware of the conclusions to which our mind leaps.

HOW TO LEAD WHAT MATTERS MOST

In February of 2021, people across Texas got a big shock. As if the winter Covid-19 surge weren't enough trouble, the state was hit with the coldest winter storm in recorded history. Temperatures in Austin dropped to as low as two or three degrees Fahrenheit. The power grid almost failed statewide, and many homes and businesses were without light and heat for days. Since deep freezes are unusual in the region, there was little infrastructure for clearing roads, which made it dangerous to go looking for supplies. It was a situation in which millions of people had to confront the unknown.

At one grocery store in an Austin suburb, hundreds of customers were trying to stock up on anything they could get for their families before the roads shut down. The store is run by H-E-B, a highly regarded chain in the region with a strong culture of preparedness. In December of 2019, months before the Covid-19 pandemic caused nationwide lockdowns in the United States, they had already identified the threat of the virus and were taking steps to prepare their stores for what was coming. They were as prepared as they could have been for the deep freeze storm, which means they were very aware of what they knew and what they were unable to know, such as what would happen if they had a store full of customers and the power went out.

Inside the store, Tim Hennessy and his wife were trying to get what they needed to survive whatever the "historically crazy weather" would bring when suddenly the store's power failed. Auxiliary lighting flickered on, and people continued shopping. Somewhere near the front of the store, a manager had to make a decision.

H-E-B has avoided publicizing the event, but Hennessy and others have shared what happened next. Let's put this story in the terms of question six: What didn't the manager know?

Without power, the checkout computers were down. How would checkers ring up the customers' purchases? Would the power come back on soon? Could they ask people to wait while they rebooted everything? The roads were bad and getting worse. Should they tell everyone to leave their carts and go home? If they did, where would people get food for their families?

Given all the unknowns, the manager had to go with what was known: H-E-B's values include doing what matters most to their customers and their community. At that moment, what mattered most was getting people stocked up and home safely.

The shoppers didn't know that the checkout was down when they heard an employee ask all customers to bring their shopping carts to the front of the store.

According to Hennessy and other customers who posted on social media, they were told to take what they had in their carts without paying and to be safe driving home.

The manager's decision went viral around the world. H-E-B was already a highly regarded company, but after that story was shared, their customer loyalty and employee pride soared. The value of that loyalty, of the reputation for doing the right thing in the face of great unknowns, was worth many times more than the value of the customers' grocery receipts that day.

PRACTICE NOTICING WHAT YOU DON'T KNOW

A new vice president of operations at a distribution center wanted to make a strong impression on his first day. He couldn't understand why productivity at the facility was so bad, so he decided to go have a look. As he was touring the loading docks with the plant manager, he noticed a man leaning on a wall. The dock was full of workers and he seized the opportunity to show everyone he meant business. So he walked up to the man and asked, "How much money do you make a week?"

"I make about $200 a week," the man said. "Why?"

The VP pulled $200 cash out of his pocket and said, "Here's a week's pay, now GET OUT and don't come back!"

Feeling pretty good about his first firing, the VP looked around and asked, "Does anyone want to tell me what that slacker did here?"

The plant manager leaned over and said, gingerly, "He's the pizza delivery guy."

When we think we know, we make fools of ourselves.

We make so many cognitive assumptions that it's sometimes hard to know what we think, let alone what we know. Zen masters teach not knowing as an important trait in being able to clearly see the world we live in. Radical self-awareness calls us to be more specific: What do we think we know, and what are we sure we don't know? And what's the difference? It's OK not to know everything—the danger is in believing that you do. Being honest about what you don't know is actually the best way toward knowing it.

We have to ask *What don't I know?* and we have to ask this question as often as we can.

HOW
does this
FEEL?

One must always be aware, to notice even
though the cost of noticing is to be responsible.

—THYLIAS MOSS

QUESTION SIX IS ABOUT MAKING sure your head is on straight. Question seven is about your heart.

Your heart and your gut make up the nerve centers in your solar plexus. What do they tell you about the moment you are in? What can those feelings teach you?

One legacy of the Age of Reason in eighteenth-century Europe is the idea that we should not trust our feelings, that we should only trust our intellect. But as we learned from Daniel Kahneman, our intellect is easily compromised with a variety of cognitive biases. A second legacy of the Age of Reason is that we equate feelings with emotions and see emotions as being unreliable. Some of the ideas promoted during the Age of Reason stuck, and they still influence the way we think about our feelings today. We assume that if we are happy, we're doing things right, so if we feel sad, we should still smile and do our jobs. But human beings, like all other animals and plants, have a large stockpile of sensory devices that we can use to feel, evaluate, and understand any situation, and these senses serve very important functions. Question seven asks you to check in with your senses.

HOW WE FEEL THE WORLD AROUND US

We can apply lots of qualifiers to the information our senses give us: we feel good or bad; the situation feels right or wrong; the moment feels safe or unsafe. As we move through this chapter, let's try to avoid value judgments. For now let's just ask whether, in the moment, a feeling is *positive* or *negative*.

Our bodies evolved as elaborate sensory devices to help us survive life in the grasslands of East Africa. In his book *Sapiens*, Yuval Noah Harari summarizes the unique history of the animals that evolved into you and me. "We don't know exactly where and when animals that can be classified as Homo sapiens first evolved from some earlier type of humans, but most scientists agree that by 150,000 years ago, East Africa was populated by Sapiens that looked a lot like us."

Sapiens had a well-developed sense of the natural world around them. Their lives depended on it. You and I are here today because somewhere, long ago, we had an ancestor who could sense when the tall grass was moving because of a gentle breeze (let's call that positive) and when it was moving because of a stalking lion (definitely negative). Among the many ways our ancestor knew positive from negative grass movement was the phenomenon of feeling the hair on the back of her neck stand up.

I thought about that ancestor one day as I was walking along the edge of a meadow with my dog Dodger. We were approaching an old live oak tree, and just as we reached the drip line, I felt the hair on my neck activate. I whispered to Dodger, "Be still." We were being watched, and if we were very quiet, we might see something interesting.

We stepped forward under the canopy of the tree, and there, ten feet up in the center of the trunk, in a knothole where a limb had long ago been removed, a face peered out. It was a small screech owl. We looked at each other for a few moments, and she let me take a picture. Looking up at the owl, I wondered how it is that, even after all these millennia removed from the plains of Africa, Homo sapiens can still sense when we are being watched.

We have all the tools to sense our environments and our feelings. And yet, how often do we use them? How good, really, are we at identifying what's happening around us or even within us?

We should be able to navigate complex exterior and interior situations with always-on clarity. And yet, we struggle. Why? Why can't we get to that sense of who we're being and who we want to be in the moment-by-moment flow of our daily lives? If we've got a world-class awareness mechanism, why are we often bad at accurately sensing what is happening within us and within those around us?

BEING ESSENTIAL BEGINS AND ENDS WITH THIS QUESTION

You are reading this book and developing this practice because you had a feeling—a sense—that it would bring you value. No one has ever had an intellectual deduction that they needed to develop radical self-awareness, at least not until the thought was triggered by a feeling that something was missing in their life or in their relationships.

Being Essential depends on deepening our capacity to use our sensory tools so we can be better equipped to notice what's going on internally and in the world around us. We find validation of our self-awareness not by asking *What do I think?* but by asking *How do I feel?* This question gets us out of our heads and into our hearts, out of our minds and into our kinesthetic senses.

The reason we save this question for the end of the practice is to bring us back to the starting point. A feeling sparked your attention, causing you to ask *Where am I?* and shoot through the questions. Now that you've gone through them all, how does it feel? If the feeling hasn't changed, then where are you?

After you've gone through the seven questions, how does it feel? If the feeling that sparked the questions hasn't changed, then where are you?

Being Essential is not an intellectual exercise. It's a full-body encounter with yourself in the present moment. It's heart, mind, and gut forcing you to full attention of who you are in your Essential Self.

Why is this question so critical? The best answer is that we spend most of our time in an internal dialogue with our

Synthetic Self, and therefore, we struggle to answer what should be the most basic of questions: *How does this feel?*

WHEN TOUGH DECISIONS *SEEM* RIGHT BUT DON'T FEEL GOOD

In my coaching work, when we run through the seven questions in a linear format—and if the person I'm working with has been able to break through their psyche and get real about whatever it is we're working through—asking *How does this feel?* usually provokes a clear answer.

Let's say you're working through some relationship issues. After using the Being Essential framework to make a big decision (let's say your partner has asked you to live with them), you're not getting a positive feeling. Perfect! So where are you? Are you ready for cohabitating? Are you with a person you want to dedicate yourself to? Maybe you just like your life as it is? Even when we believe we have made a logical decision using a thought framework, we sometimes can lead ourselves to the wrong answer. If we practice self-awareness, we can sense our Essential Self telling us to think again. Living with our partner may make sense, but if it doesn't feel right, we must listen to that bodily alert and keep asking the questions. Every time you work through the problem, it gets easier to solve.

Sometimes we must work through a situation that feels fearful or causes us a sense of loss. But as you work through the process, you probably know how you feel even before you get to the last question. You know because you felt yourself let go right at question four: *What do I want?* I want to stop feeling afraid or feeling unloved. I want to pivot to action and appreciation. I want to let go of the fear. And so you let go.

How does it feel? Good. Liberating. Energizing. Joyful. (All positive feelings.) You can live in those feelings until the next time a difficult emotion locks in and you have to process it again. And each time you do, it gets easier and faster. The more you practice, the less your negative feelings can hold on to you.

I was working with a client we'll call Chris, one of the most brilliant leaders I've ever met. He had been working for about a year at a retail chain and was charged with creating business intelligence: an operating system for the stores, the supply chain, and the customer relationships, beginning with automating manual processes. It took other leaders a while to understand what he was offering, but when they got it, they started swamping him with critical requests for solutions. There was so much work to do that he had a backlog of more than six months of projects, with frequent triage meetings to decide which projects were the most critical and could deliver the most return on time invested.

It was exhilarating. It was also exhausting.

In the middle of all that, the company was looking for a new chief technology officer to take over the design and management of all the technological platforms that the company ran on, from point-of-sale to accounting to inventory management. One day the CEO said to Chris, "Hey, why don't you take on both roles?"

We discussed the CEO's offer in Chris's next coaching session.

"OK," Chris said, explaining why he thought this was such an unworkable idea, "I can see the logic of managing both sides of the technology issues—platforms and solutions. But I'm already stressed to the limit and these solutions we're developing are critical to everything we're trying to do. If I take my focus off them to manage the two departments, everything is going to suffer. I don't see any way this works."

We used the Being Essential seven questions to work through both the reality of the issues and how he felt about them. When we got to the last question, Chris was still troubled.

"I just can't get there," he said. "It doesn't feel right."

And so we went through it all again, weighing pros and cons and imagining alternative scenarios. I had no opinion. I could see both sides of the issue and certainly understood where Chris was coming from. This was not an easy decision, and there were serious pitfalls in both absorbing the CTO position and sticking with just one role.

But when we got to the fifth question again, *What wants to happen?* I suddenly saw with profound clarity that only one choice made sense for the long term: what he was creating—the "digital operating system" for the entire company—had to be designed and managed in a holistic fashion. It had to be in one department. About forty seconds later, Chris's eyes widened, and he sighed.

"I just saw it," he said. "I have to do this. It's the only way it works." He had seen the same thing I saw—that he had to manage the whole. He would have to weather the management challenges of merging the two departments and keep the business intelligence projects moving forward, too. We worked on a plan for him to manage his time and resources to get the job done. We talked about who he could charge with innovation duties to keep the solutions moving and who would be essential to helping him organize the technology side of the house to bring the two departments together. We thought it would take about six months of hard work to get there, but that once they got through the transition, everything would work better. And we were right.

When we met for coaching after the fourth month, things were really tough. We had to talk about firing a couple of people who just couldn't make the transition. I could see the stress on his face. But when we met a month later, Chris was smiling. I asked him what had happened.

"I don't know," he said. "A couple of weeks ago, everyone just got it. We all understood why this was important and we quit fighting about it. And suddenly, it's all working."

How does it feel? "It feels great. This was the right way to go." By accessing his Essential Self when he saw what wanted to happen, he achieved the leadership thinking he needed to make the transition. This didn't mean that the change was seamless or easy, but the connection Chris was able to make—knowing that he must plug the two departments into one operating unit—was so clear that, even under stress, he knew he was on the right track. He trusted the feeling, and his trust paid off for everyone involved.

The lesson here is that you will experience situations where the right answer does not feel positive, at least not at first. Change can be scary, and new roles will be challenging. Use the questions to work through your feelings, but never stop asking, *How does this feel?* This question is not complicated: it either feels positive or it doesn't. If it does, move forward. If it doesn't, keep working. You will get there, even if some situations take more work than others.

LEADING WITH FEELING

We owe our existence as human beings to our innate ability to sense the world around us, to sense the people we live and work with, and to sense ourselves. Those senses, along with other social attributes, kept us flourishing as we spread from Africa to populate the entire world. Whether we know it or not, our sensing abilities are just as important today as they ever were.

We may not need to sense lions in the bush, but we've all had the experience of being in a room and sensing someone was looking at us. How do we sense that? Cognitive scientists call this "gaze detection" and know that the reaction it creates in the brain is very precise. If the person looking at you turns her gaze just a degree or two away from you, the brain cells that were activated quiet down. While the specific cells responsible for this effect have not been identified in the human brain, more than 800 studies have been published by biologists studying gaze detection in macaque monkeys. Scientists have discovered the neurological circuits responsible for gaze, right down to the specific section of the monkey's brain. (It's the ventral premotor region F5, in case you were interested.)

Sensing the gaze and other cues from those around us is important in our professional lives as well. When you're running a meeting, you need to sense the attention of others at the table. If you sense that the people at the table are withdrawing from the conversation, you can ask them where they are. Keep asking until the energy feels positive again.

Noticing how you feel is not about some psychic experience. In fact, there is a scientific explanation for how we sense ourselves in relation to others. Our brains—and animal brains—have mirror neurons that seem to reflect and communicate the inner state of those around us. In a paper published in 2013 that surveyed all the current studies, James Kilner and Roger Lemon of University College of Medicine in London shared the importance of these studies.

"For us," they wrote, "the discovery of mirror neurons was exciting because it has led to a new way of thinking about how we generate our own actions and how we monitor and interpret the actions of others. This discovery prompted the notion that, from a functional viewpoint, action, execution, and observation are closely-related processes, and indeed that our ability to interpret the actions of others requires the involvement of our own motor system."

Marco Iacoboni at UCLA has reported that mirror neurons may help the human brain read and understand the actions of others. In a 2005 study, Iacoboni and his team reported that mirror neurons could help us read intention. Subjects watching a person pick up a teacup could identify in advance whether she planned to sip from it or was just clearing the table. He suggested that mirror neurons might form the basis for our ability to feel empathy for others. We are hardwired to read all the social cues in a room and so, at least technically, have all the tools we need for strong social intelligence. But it only works if we are radically aware of how we feel in the moment and skilled at sensing how our companions feel as well.

You can't be an effective leader if you are weak on sensing the people around you. And you can't be strong on sensing others if you are weak on sensing yourself. This is the practice that will give you the profound ability to know yourself, to know others, and to know what's appropriate in the moment.

How does that feel?

FINDING THE HEART
of the PRACTICE

It is only with the heart that one can see rightly;
what is essential is invisible to the eye.

—ANTOINE DE SAINT-EXUPÉRY

SO FAR WE'VE SPOKEN MOSTLY about the mind and the dualistic structure of the Synthetic Self and the Essential Self. There's one more thing we have to consider in Being Essential, and that is the power of the heart. When you are aware of where your heart is, asking question seven, *How does this feel?* becomes your touchstone. If your heart is not right, your mind cannot be either. The heart is the engine that drives your sense of well-being. The practice of Being Essential is closely tied to the wellness of the heart and the type of energy it radiates in the world. So, before we close, let's take a moment to explore this connection and what it means for your work to find radical self-awareness.

You can think of the heart as a virtually unlimited nuclear energy storage system that can power whichever mind is running your ship. Just as the mind exists in both temporal and transcendent spheres, so does the heart. On one hand, it provides the physical body with a heartbeat. On the other hand, it provides the power to either blow up your world or light up your life. In Hindu and Buddhist systems, this energy center is called the heart chakra or *anahata*.

Recent research shows that the heart's electromagnetic field reaches as much as three feet outside your body and is five thousand times more powerful than that of your brain. In fact, it appears that the heart sends more information to the brain than the brain sends to the heart. Your heart's electromagnetic field can be detected in an electro-cardiogram of a person sitting beside you. When you come close to another person, your heart's force field causes a change in them. This research is important in helping us to understand the power our heart has and how it affects our state of being. When we are in a positive mindset, we create harmonious patterns in the heart's energy field that lead to what scientists call *coherence*. According to Dr. Rollin McCraty, research director at the Heartmath Institute, "Coherence is the state when the heart, mind, and emotions are in energetic alignment and cooperation. It is a state that builds resilience." In that state of calm focus and presence, the researchers find that we are better at learning, that we make better choices because we can see a wider selection of options in front of us.

When the Synthetic Self is dominant, it draws on the heart's energy to create fear and rage, powering the extreme emotions of upset. On the other hand, when your Essential Self is running the show, it draws on the heart to generate feelings of well-being, possibility, and joy. In its healthy state, the heart radiates positive energy, a state we know as being "open-hearted." When we are open-hearted, we are able to accept and appreciate what is happening in our world and in the people around us. We radiate a positive field. But when the heart is ruled by the Synthetic Self, the heart's energy is characterized by feelings of fear and unworthiness. Because the Synthetic Self suppresses those feelings, the energy of the heart can become blocked. If you have learned to resist feelings to protect your Synthetic Self, then the energy has nowhere to go. It curls up and goes deep into your heart, pent-up power waiting for release.

The practice of Being Essential is designed to clear not only the mind but also the blocked energy of the heart. As you practice the questions, you clear your heart and mind and become more adept at returning to the Essential Self, more skilled at clearing out the blockages that are getting in the way of your awareness of yourself and how you are showing up in your role as a leader.

LEAD FROM THE ESSENTIAL HEART

You probably at some point have encountered a leader who was unbalanced, who led from fear and upset, who trusted no one, and who played people in the organization against each other. Under such a leader, it's likely that the best people will leave the organization, the least effective people will rise, and the middle-performers usually tolerate an unsatisfying career path until they finally resign or retire. Leaders like this, who lead from the Synthetic Self, might get things done, but their teams are not fulfilled—and, likely, neither are they if they're being honest.

At our emotional core, there are only two emotions: love and fear. Every other emotion you can name is constructed from one or the other. One is always healing and the other is always harming. Self-aware leaders know in their hearts when they are acting from love or from fear. They are able to sense a feeling of upset and identify that they are acting from their Synthetic Self. From that awareness, they have any combination of the seven questions that they can use to shift to their Essential Self, to pivot to a place of joy and positive expectations. The practice of Being Essential, then, is to develop the radical self-awareness to know where you are and why you are there. The heart will always tell you when you need to revisit the process and realign your mind.

Remember, we create the world inside our minds. We take the whole of the world outside us and build a model of it inside our minds, and that's where we live. In that construction, we build our Synthetic Self to keep our ego safe.

We pay a terrible price for this because, as we suppress our energy out of fear, we impede the heart's ability to heal us.

At the same time, we have an Essential Self that can see what we're doing, knows the negative feelings and behaviors are unsupportable, and is calling on us to step out of the false world we've built. It sees the disturbances we create within our minds and takes an objective view of it.

We can live in either mind, but we can only transcend our experience in the mind of the Essential Self. When we are in that mind, we can see our duality and what is causing it. When we are in the mind of the Synthetic Self, we lack self-awareness. The energy of the heart offers a way out. As we learned when we looked at question seven, we can identify which mind we are in by noticing the way we feel. When we are aware of the feeling of our heart, we can use the heart's energy to help us power the mindset change we need. The heart will reward us with feelings of coherence, of joy, and of well-being.

WHERE ARE YOU IN YOUR HEART?

In Martin Buber's story from the chapter on question one, the jailed rabbi reminds the chief of police that God asks each of us, "Where are you?"

"When asking in this manner," Buber goes on to suggest, "God wishes to effect something in a person that can only be effected by such a question. The question is intended to penetrate the human heart but can do so only if the person allows the heart to be penetrated." The Synthetic Self depends for its very existence on keeping the heart impenetrable. The Essential Self, on the other hand, is all heart. It exists in relationship to a healthy heart. If the heart is blocked, the Essential Self will work around the blockage to release the energy. The seven questions are the workaround.

Let's look at an example. Remember a time when you anticipated a conflict—a terrible feeling of impending doom, especially when important work is at hand. Maybe you think that your colleagues blame your team for holding up the project, or they feel that your management has been sloppy. Your heart races as your mind spins a story where you are criticized or seen as an ineffective leader. The stress of anticipation consumes your thoughts, and it's hard to focus on your goals, which only exacerbates the feeling.

So, who are you being?

Ah, you think. *I am being fearful. I am thinking and acting from a fearful heart. And I don't want that, do I? What I want is an open and joyful heart.* So you let go of that fear and, literally, turn your self around, from being Synthetic to being Essential.

Will it work every time? Yes, with practice. It's like anything else we work on in life. The heart and mind are like muscles that grow stronger with exercise and training.

There are a thousand things that can trigger fear and upset. It happens so often and at a low enough frequency that we don't even notice. Anxiety can become our baseline.

Your mind fixates on the report you haven't finished, the call you didn't return, the promise you are definitely going to keep but haven't quite gotten to yet. And, oh yeah, your to-do list! Which seems to grow longer rather than shorter each day.

It doesn't take long before the anxious baseline triggers an outburst and you get angry at your spouse or your child or your goldfish. You just lose it. But the upsets don't have to own you, and with practice you can minimize and eventually eliminate them, replacing them with amused curiosity: *Look at me, I almost got upset there. Why did I go there?*

I like to say there are four levels of mastery of the heart.

Level 1, the highest: We see the event that would once have triggered upset, but it sails right past us without effect and we laugh at it.

Level 2: We feel the vibration of the upset, but it doesn't hook us and we are free from it and grateful that we've done the practice.

Level 3: The upset hooks us, but we detach quickly and let it go.

And Level 4: You have to send flowers and a note of apology for your actions. But that's all right; you're learning.

With each level, your ability to let go of the things that get in the way of self-awareness improves. You feel anxiety in your heart, you connect the anxiety to an upcoming meeting that you worry might result in conflict, and you just let go of the anxiety. You release the energy from your heart. And guess what? When you get to the meeting, you feel fine and don't gravitate toward conflict or appear defensive. Instead, your self-awareness defuses the energy and you lead the group to a positive outcome.

The power of the heart is its ability to communicate your Essential Self to those around you, just by the way they experience you and your energy.

THE GIFT *of* RADICAL SELF-AWARENESS

What great leaders have in common is that
each truly knows his or her strengths—and can
call on the right strength at the right time.

—DONALD O. CLIFTON

WE'VE LEARNED THAT EACH ONE of us has complete access to a high degree of awareness of who we are being. The irony is that most of the time we are unaware of our awareness. In part, that's because we are wired for unawareness by evolution. We would not be here today if early Homo sapiens sat around all day, engaged in the story of who they were and why they were alive. Navel gazing, although related to the general area of the stomach, does not fill us up. We evolved by focusing on practical matters, hunting and gathering the day's food, collecting water, making tools and other useful objects. Our success as a species has been built on our ability to keep moving and not think too much about the damage we cause. We are provided with the lizard mind of the amygdala, which helps us sense and react to danger without having to do too much math. We sense the danger and we jump. We jump and we don't ask why.

Not that we haven't had people giving serious thought to the nature of human consciousness and how our minds can work both for us and against us. As we've seen through the examples of this book, the study of the mind is quite ancient. The Hindu Vedic texts, which influenced Buddhism and Zen, go back thousands of years and echo some of the most advanced cognitive science of today, as well as ideas in quantum physics. The most ancient Hebrew texts, which influenced Christian and Muslim thought, go back nearly as far and are still deeply relevant to our knowledge of how our minds work and what kind of thinking can make them work better. And then there were the Greeks and the Chinese—Aristotle and Lao Tsu, to name just two—whose writings on the nature of the mind still resonate thousands of years beyond their own lives.

The only questions that really matter are the ones you ask yourself.

—URSULA K. LE GUIN

LEADERSHIP IS AT A CROSSROADS

There has never been a time when a single leader could make such a dramatic difference in our world because there has never been a time when human beings have been so connected. Think about this one fact: the Covid-19 pandemic was the first time in the history of the human species when not only every society was going through the same experience of suffering, but every society knew that all the rest of humanity was enduring the same experience.

You would think that the experience of being united in a global outbreak would bring us together, as space alien films have predicted could happen for so long. And yet, we have never been so divided. East versus west. North versus south. Red versus blue. White versus Black. Us versus them.

In the classic 1950s sci-fi series *The Twilight Zone*, there's an episode that presaged this moment. The episode "To Serve Man" features a visit to Earth by a race of nine-foot-tall aliens. They have arrived to provide humanitarian aid by sharing advanced technology with earthlings. As a gift, they offer a book in their own language. Its title: *To Serve Man*. Impressed by the selfless sentiment, and with all of Earth's most pressing problems solved by the visitors and world peace at hand, a delegation of humans boards a spaceship for a goodwill visit to their benefactors' home planet. Suddenly, a member of the translation team comes running up to the ship. Restrained by alien guards, she can only shout a warning.

"Don't get on that ship! The rest of the book, *To Serve Man*, it's . . . IT'S A COOKBOOK!"

Today, in societies around the world, we are jumping out of the fires we have lit and into the frying pans of our own devices. Instead of leading, we are feeding on each other, reverting to tribalism even when we know we should cooperate. We need leadership that takes a world view—a universal view—of what acts would serve the continued existence of our human species and which will hasten our demise.

WE NEED LEADERSHIP THAT REPRESENTS THE BEST OF WHAT IT MEANS TO BE A HUMAN BEING.

We need leadership that represents the best of what it means to be a human being. Fortunately, we have that leadership. In all lines of endeavor, in every society. In commerce, government, and education. In the arts and sciences. On the oceans, in space, and on every continent, we have women and men who are working hard to expand the good we have done in the last century or two in reducing poverty, expanding universal education, and improving health outcomes.

Your life expectancy and mine is twice what it was when the last global pandemic hit us a century ago, and we know so much more about our fundamental interconnectedness as human beings. About our increasingly precarious place in the system of life on this planet. And about the idea that the entire known universe might amount to more than a sky full of flaming rocks in the vast emptiness of space, and nine billion human beings tucked onto a single planet.

We need leadership that sees beyond next year's election cycle and next quarter's business results. We need leadership that sees the close-up picture in the lives of individual families and communities and the wide-angle view of the broad system of life, leadership that is conscious of where we are now and of the responsibilities we have to each other.

We need leadership, within ourselves, that is focused on what matters most, focused on Being Essential.

HOW MANY QUESTIONS DO YOU NEED?

Earlier we talked about using the questions in an order that makes sense for a given situation and about how sometimes we only need certain questions to help us realign to Being Essential. Now, how do you know which questions to use, and how many do you need to reconnect with the Essential Self?

My answer: You need however many of the questions it takes to get where you need to be—and where you need to be is balanced, open-hearted, and leading from your Essential Self. The Being Essential process is totally customizable. There may be times when the source of the imbalance isn't clear to you and you need to take the full journey of seven questions. But more and more, you will find that just noticing how you feel—where your heart is—will instantly trigger the shift you want to make. If the shift isn't instant, then at least it happens more easily than before you began the practice. You will get better at it.

This is a practice. It would be wonderful if you could read a book on how to dance and then walk onto the floor and perform the tango. But that's not how it works. Learning anything takes practice. And practice takes commitment.

It comes down to this: Do you want to be happy?

Getting the promotion to the CEO's chair. Getting the seat on the company jet. Looking at your house on the lake and counting your money. None of these things will necessarily make you open-hearted or self-aware. You don't need any of them to be happy.

You must decide who you want to be. What does happy look like for you?

Each of us has access to full awareness of who we are being and why. The irony is that most of the time we are unaware of our awareness.

The most valuable possession
you can own is an open heart.

—CARLOS SANTANA

WHERE ARE YOU NOW, AND WHERE DO YOU WANT TO GO?

The other morning, I was writing in my journal, making a note about how I felt. "I like how I feel right now," I wrote. But when I looked at it, my fingers had typed "feel *fight* now." Hmmm, Freudian alert! So I took a moment to think about where my mind was when that happened, and I saw that the answer is simple. There is and will always be a part of me deep down that thinks life is a struggle. And sometimes it is. So I acknowledged that fearful voice and invited it to go back to sleep. I am not going to be guided by that fear.

We have a choice in every moment. We can choose who we are being. But we can only access that choice if we are *aware* of who we are being. Everything comes from that. Everything worth doing, everything worth having, everything worth sharing. What could matter more than who you are as a person?

Being Essential is not a formula or a process. It's a practice, a constant practice of calling yourself back to now, to this present moment, and checking on where your awareness is. Like any other art, the more you practice it, the more natural and beautiful it becomes.

Ask yourself who you are when you are at your best. What does it feel like to be you at that moment? What if you could extend that moment to last your whole life? And what if you could be the kind of person who could lead others to live at their best? At work, at home, at any moment, Being Essential.

You've got this. So, *be* it.

I know that people can be better than they are. We are capable of bearing a great burden, once we discover that the burden is reality and arrive where reality is.

—JAMES BALDWIN

ACKNOWLEDGMENTS

MY LIFE AND MY WORK have been shaped and defined by teachers who have helped me understand myself so that I might understand others. It's a long list that begins with my oldest friend, Dr. Sat-Kaur Khalsa. Over the years, her gentle guidance has taught me who I was being and when I was holding myself back. The many writers and teachers she has pointed me to have given me a foundation on which I have built my own work.

Dr. Frank Allen came into my life following the leadership incident I shared in the opening chapter and has been my coach for the past decade and a half. His humor and mastery have helped me grow as a thinker and teacher and made me a better coach. His writings inspire me, and his presence is a powerful reminder of what it means to be in the moment.

Kevin and Jackie Freiberg have helped me guide leaders

of client companies for years, and they gave me the opportunity to collaborate with them on *Nanovation*, truly a great honor. Their friendship, vision, and wisdom inspire me to approach life with guts, and their early comments on this work appear in several places in the book.

I began to develop the Being Essential framework in 2018 in a series of talks I gave to corporate clients. I'm grateful to David Murray, of the Professional Speechwriters Association, for the many moments of grace he and I have shared over the years. Every time he's put me in front of an audience has helped me develop my work. David also introduced me to my publisher, Disruption Books.

In 2018, while directing a corporate event in Rome, I met my friend Emanuele Faini, a consultant in the hotel industry and one of the city's top pasta makers, who told me that he read Martin Buber's *The Way of Man* once a year. When he sent me a copy of the book, I discovered the first question—*Where are you?*—on the first page of the first chapter in Buber's work and knew it would be the foundation of my own.

That question and the idea of locating where we are led me to the work of Elizabeth Kapu'uwailani Lindsey, who spent years studying the wayfaring traditions of Micronesia. The understanding of "self-navigation" as the core of radical self-awareness was critical to my work and I am grateful for the time she has spent helping me. Check out her TEDx talk!

In early 2019 David Murray and Lucinda Holdforth of the University of Sydney invited me to conduct the first

Being Essential workshop at the Asia-Pacific Speechwriters Conference in Sydney. I'm grateful to them for the opportunity to get this work on its feet, and I'm grateful to the brilliant speechwriters who wholeheartedly dug into the work with me.

Sharing the work defines the work, and so I'm grateful to the many friends and colleagues who read early drafts and shared their wise counsel. Sille Østergaard in New York and Murry Steinman in Bozeman gave me great notes and support in early 2020, as did my coaching colleagues Herb Dyer of Austin and Janis Apted of Houston.

Anyone who attempts the awesome challenge of writing a book appreciates all the help they can get, and I am honored by many writer friends who gave me support and encouragement, including Steve Soltis, Charles McNair, Bijoy Goswami, Frank Spinelli, and Jon Dunkelberger. Their belief in the project kept me going, as did the enthusiasm of my coaching clients who have worked through problems in their organizations with the Being Essential framework.

Over the past few years, I've seen many of my clients rise to positions of great responsibility and personal growth. Two in particular gave me great joy. After spending my career coaching people in senior positions, I've been working with next-generation leaders, some as young as twenty-five. When two of them told me that this work had changed their lives, I felt complete. Meg and Dominic, you know who you are.

In particular, I want to thank my colleagues in Reservoir LLC, beginning with Eric McNulty at Harvard and Mark

Lipton at The New School and Parsons. Their friendship and guidance over the years have been a profound gift. They are also the authors of great books on leadership and I urge you to check them out.

Also with Reservoir, my colleague and friend Inna Ulanova provided unwavering support with her belief in this book. She may be the smartest person I've ever had the pleasure of working with and is a trusted counsel in everything we do. As my closest business colleague and one of my dearest friends, she has been a driving force in both the completion of the manuscript and the journey through its publishing.

And that brings me to my publisher and editor, Kris Pauls of Disruption Books. Her immediate support of and appreciation for the book sold me on working with her, and her insight in helping me restructure and rewrite the manuscript made a huge difference. Thanks to Janet Potter for her brilliant marketing help in bringing the book to the attention of the industry and book buyers. To Ellen Bitterman, my favorite copy editor, for her care in cleaning up the writing. To Inna for the author's photo, and to the amazing Blake Hines for photo editing. And many thanks to my multitalented friend, Tom Dobson, for directing and producing the audiobook edition of *Being Essential*.

And finally, thanks go to one more person, my beloved wife and partner of thirty years, Jean Compton. Jean listened to every chapter and shared her thoughts and wisdom every step of the way. Her patience and support kept me moving forward, and I appreciate her love and partnership so much.

REFERENCES

LOOKING INTO THE MIND OF A LEADER

Campbell, Joseph. *The Hero with a Thousand Faces*. New York: Pantheon Books, 1968.

Dunston, Dain. *The Downside of Up: A Comic Novel of Outrageous Fortune*. Scotts Valley: Vernacular Press, 2014.

Freiberg, Kevin, Jackie Freiberg, and Dain Dunston. *Nanovation: How a Little Car Can Teach the World to Think Big and Act Bold*. Nashville: Thomas Nelson, 2012.

THE SEARCH FOR THE ESSENTIAL SELF

Allen, Frank E., and Kathleen Allen-Weber. *Changing Minds: Recognition (A Journey of Awakening)*. Independently published, 2019.

Damasio, Antonio R. "How the Brain Creates the Mind." *Scientific American*, December 1999. https://www.scientificamerican .com/article/how-the-brain-creates-the-mind/.

Harari, Yuval Noah. *Sapiens: A Brief History of Humankind*. New York: Harper, 2015.

Haven, Kendall. *Story Proof: The Science Behind the Startling Power of Story*. Santa Barbara: Libraries Unlimited, 2007.

Leonard, Elmore. *The Switch: A Novel*. Bantam Books, 1978.

THE PRACTICE OF RADICAL SELF-AWARENESS

Dare to Think Like a Champion Today. TEDxUND, 2018. https ://www.ted.com/talks/amber_selking_dare_to_think _like_a_champion_today.

Eurich, Tasha. "What Self-Awareness Really Is (and How to Cultivate It)." *Harvard Business Review*, January 4, 2018. https ://hbr.org/2018/01/what-self-awareness-really-is-and-how -to-cultivate-it.

Finzi, Benjamin, Mark Lipton, Kathy Lu, and Vincent Firth. "Emotional Fortitude: The Inner Work of the CEO." Deloitte Insights, July 9, 2020. https://www2.deloitte.com /us/en/insights/topics/leadership/ceo-decision-making -emotional-fortitude.html.

Maslow, Abraham H. "Peak Experiences as Acute Identity Experiences." *The American Journal of Psychoanalysis* 21 (1961): 254–62. https://doi.org/10.1007/bf01873126.

Seligman, Martin E. P. *Learned Optimism: How to Change Your Mind and Your Life*. New York: Vintage Books, 2006.

V (formerly Eve Ensler). *The Apology*. London: Bloomsbury Publishing, 2019.

EMBRACING YOUR ESSENTIAL CHILD

Ray, Michael. *The Highest Goal: The Secret That Sustains You in Every Moment*. Oakland: Berrett-Koehler Publishers, 2005.

QUESTION 1: WHERE ARE YOU?

Buber, Martin. *The Way of Man: According to the Teaching of Hasidism*. Woodstock, VT: Jewish Lights, 2012.

QUESTION 2: WHY ARE YOU HERE?

Boyle, Gregory. *Tattoos on the Heart: The Power of Boundless Compassion*. New York: Free Press, 2011.

Tredinnick, Mark. *Egret in a Ploughed Field*. Hong Kong: The Chinese University of Hong Kong Press, 2018.

Vyasa, Veda. *The Bhagavad Gita*. Translated by Eknath Easwaran. 2nd ed. Tomales, CA: Nilgiri Press, 2007.

QUESTION 3: WHO ARE YOU BEING?

Smith, Kerri. "Neuroscience vs Philosophy: Taking Aim at Free Will." *Nature* 477, no. 7362 (2011): 23–25. https://doi.org/10.1038/477023a.

QUESTION 4: WHAT DO YOU WANT?

Snyder, Blake. *Save the Cat! Strikes Back: More Trouble for Screenwriters to Get into . . . and Out Of.* Save the Cat! Press, 2009.

QUESTION 5: WHAT WANTS TO HAPPEN?

Isaacson, Walter. *The Innovators: How a Group of Hackers, Geniuses, and Geeks Created the Digital Revolution.* New York: Simon & Schuster, 2015.

Jung, Carl. *Synchronicity: An Acausal Connecting Principle.* Translated by Richard Francis Carrington Hull. Princeton, NJ: Princeton University Press, 2010.

Jung, Carl, and Wolfgang Pauli. *Atom and Archetype: The Pauli/Jung Letters, 1932-1958.* Edited by Carl Alfred Meier. Translated by David Roscoe. Princeton, NJ: Princeton University Press, 2014.

Ramo, Joshua Cooper. *The Seventh Sense: Power, Fortune, and Survival in the Age of Networks.* Boston: Little, Brown and Company, 2016.

Senge, Peter M., C. Otto Scharmer, Joseph Jaworski, and Betty Sue Flowers. *Presence: Human Purpose and the Field of the Future.* New York: Currency, 2008.

von Franz, Marie-Louise. *On Divination and Synchronicity: The Psychology of Meaningful Chance.* Scarborough, Ontario: Inner City Books, 1980.

Yoshikawa, Eiji. *Musashi: An Epic Novel of the Samurai Era.* Translated by Charles Terry. Tokyo: Kodansha, 2012.

QUESTION 6: WHAT DON'T YOU KNOW?

Suzuki, Shunryu. *Zen Mind, Beginner's Mind: Informal Talks on Zen Meditation and Practice.* Edited by Trudy Dixon. Boulder: Shambhala, 2011.

Thinking That We Know. National Academy of Science's Sackler Colloquium, 2012. https://www.youtube.com/watch?v=di6kl4ViWgk.

QUESTION 7: HOW DOES THIS FEEL?

Harari, Yuval Noah. *Sapiens: A Brief History of Humankind.* New York: Harper, 2015.

Iacoboni, Marco, Istvan Molnar-Szakacs, Vittorio Gallese, Giovanni Buccino, John C. Mazziotta, and Giacomo Rizzolatti. "Grasping the Intentions of Others with One's Own Mirror Neuron System." *PLoS Biology* 3, no. 3 (February 22, 2005). https://doi.org/10.1371/journal.pbio.0030079.

Kilner, James Morvan, and Roger N. Lemon. "What We Know Currently about Mirror Neurons." *Current Biology* 23, no. 23 (December 2, 2013): R1057–R1062. https://doi.org/10.1016/j.cub.2013.10.051.

FINDING THE HEART OF THE PRACTICE

Harari, Yuval Noah. *Sapiens: A Brief History of Humankind.* New York: Harper, 2015.

McCraty, Rollin, Mike Atkinson, Dana Tomasino, and Raymond Trevor Bradley. "The Coherent Heart: Heart–Brain Interactions, Psychophysiological Coherence, and the Emergence of System-Wide Order." *Integral Review* 5, no. 2 (December 2009).

ABOUT *the* AUTHOR

DAIN DUNSTON has spent thirty-five years as an advisor and coach to leaders, helping them frame the foundation of their personal and professional journeys. He is a founding partner in Reservoir LLC, a coalition of executive coaches that includes some of the best minds from leading universities. Reservoir provides advisory services to the C-suite, next-generation leadership development, and advocacy for conscious leadership, societal responsibility, and sustainable business practices.

Dain is the coauthor, with Kevin and Jackie Freiberg, of *Nanovation: How a Little Car Can Teach the World to Think Big and Act Bold*. He is also the author of two novels, *The Downside of Up: A Comic Novel of Outrageous Fortune* and *The Straight Dope: A Novel of Sex, Death, and Rock & Roll*. He is a frequent speaker on leadership, culture, and coaching topics.

Dain lives in Wimberley, Texas, in the hills outside of Austin, with his wife, art dealer and writer Jean Compton, and a large standard poodle named Jackson.